BEING A ROCK
IN A HARD PLACE

BEING A ROCK IN A HARD PLACE

Facing the Challenges of Ministry

Doreen M. McFarlane

CASCADE *Books* • Eugene, Oregon

BEING A ROCK IN A HARD PLACE
Facing the Challenges of Ministry

Copyright © 2026 Doreen M. McFarlane. All rights reserved. Except for brief quotations in critical publications or reviews, no part of this book may be reproduced in any manner without prior written permission from the publisher. Write: Permissions, Wipf and Stock Publishers, 199 W. 8th Ave., Suite 3, Eugene, OR 97401.

Cascade Books
An Imprint of Wipf and Stock Publishers
199 W. 8th Ave., Suite 3
Eugene, OR 97401

www.wipfandstock.com

PAPERBACK ISBN: 979-8-3852-4282-5
HARDCOVER ISBN: 979-8-3852-4283-2
EBOOK ISBN: 979-8-3852-4284-9

Cataloguing-in-Publication data:

Names: McFarlane, Doreen M., author.
Title: Being a rock in a hard place : facing the challenges of ministry / Doreen M. McFarlane.
Description: Eugene, OR: Cascade Books, 2026.
Identifiers: ISBN 979-8-3852-4282-5 (paperback) | ISBN 979-8-3852-4283-2 (hardcover) | ISBN 979-8-3852-4284-9 (ebook)
Subjects: LCSH: Clergy—office. | Pastoral theology. | Vocation.
Classification: BV660.2 M4 2026 (print) | BV660.2 (ebook)

The Scripture quotations contained herein are from the New Revised Standard Version, Updated Edition Bible, copyright © 1989, 2021 by the Division of Christian Education of the National Council of the Churches of Christ in the U.S.A. and are used by permission. All Rights reserved.

This book is dedicated to the hundreds of pastors in our churches who are struggling with the many difficulties that arise in the context of their ministry; to all those who have learned that the realities seldom resemble the ideals with which they came into their calling. May they maintain their perspective. May they find the strength they need to move forward. And, may they always remember how very loved they are.

Contents

Preface ix

Introduction xi

SECTION ONE – Feelings

1. Called to a (not so) perfect congregation 3
2. Called but feeling annoyed 7
3. Called but feeling angry 11
4. Called but feeling overworked 15
5. Called but feeling confused 19
6. Called but feeling disjointed 24
7. Called but feeling sad 27
8. Called but feeling like a fool 34
9. Called but feeling like laughing 39
10. Called but feeling betrayed 44

SECTION TWO – Behaviors

11. Called to be friendly but not allowed a friend! 49
12. Called to love them, but I don't love that one! 53
13. Called to confidentiality, but only on my part! 57
14. Called to lead, but everybody's my boss! 60
15. Called to mission but required to "keep the lights on" 64

Contents

16. Called to a church but running a "country club" 68

17. Called to be a community leader but expected to stay in my office 71

18. Called to model for the Joneses but expected to keep up with them 75

19. Called by a search committee with an agenda other than that of the congregation 79

20. Called to those who say they support me but disappear when the chips are down 83

21. Called to be a "nice young family," but my family can't bear it! 88

22. Called to admonish, preach, and teach but expected to appease, please, and entertain 92

23. Called to console, but am I consoling a perpetrator? 95

24. Called to observe boundaries but afraid of being accused anyway! 99

SECTION THREE – Choices, Actions, and Consequences

25. How can I know for sure that I'm in the right? 105

26. What and how much am I willing to lose? 108

27. Different responses to male and female pastors 112

28. Can everybody win, and, if not, who needs to win? 117

29. Can I live with occasionally being the "bad guy"? 121

30. What if issues are "swept under the carpet"? 125

31. When the retired pastor will not leave 131

Conclusions – Thank God I am called 135

Addendum – If you feel overwhelmed 141

Preface

I believe it was at least a dozen years ago when I started writing this book. I am guessing my reason was that I was in the throes of parish ministry and pondering on the many challenging issues that were an everyday part of the kind of work I was doing. The issues were not all mine, of course. I was hearing from friends, colleagues, and acquaintances in our "business" dealing with soul-wrenching parish issues. I was also hearing over the years about too many pastors who seemed to suddenly abandon their positions (and worse). When I started writing this book, it must have been around the time that my eyes were being opened.

I recall sitting with a priest in my church's sanctuary one afternoon after an interfaith clergy gathering. (I do not at all recall his name or even which church or what year it was.) He told me how very alone he felt in parish ministry. Not realizing how sad and serious he was, I countered by saying, "Well, as a priest, you always have God to talk to." He looked sadly into my eyes and responded very firmly, "I do talk to God but God does not answer." I am not sure what response or comment I gave him, but I do recall realizing he was truly troubled and should get some help or he'd be leaving the ministry one day soon. That conversation stands out in my mind.

Now, all these years and many experiences later, I seem better equipped to understand and handle church-related issues. But I have also come to see that a book like this, one that addresses them in a practical down-to-earth manner, could be helpful for working

Preface

pastors. It will show pastors that they are, indeed, not alone. And it will help them to communicate with God and their people in a practical and honest way.

This book does not assume to solve parish life problems. It will, I sincerely hope, address their realities, and offer some perspective in handling the issues and our feelings about them with grace and courage.

With many years of ordained ministry under my belt (and still going), I can tell you this much. You can do it!

Introduction

This book is for you, the pastor. You understand that you are called by God and by a congregation, and you have been ordained by a church body. Nothing will get in the way of you being a pastor. Still, as all pastors know too well, there are those days and there are so many of them! "If only I were a better Christian, I could have felt less angry," you have probably said to yourself. "If only I could have answered her questions in more detail, then that meeting would have gone more smoothly." "If only I was better with children, that family would not have left the church." No matter how accomplished you may be as a pastor, chances are there are times when you question either your credentials, your ability to be truly compassionate, or both. The reason is that church life, although laden with blessings, can also be a minefield for the pastor! The fact is that no amount of preparation or experience can completely prepare us for the variety and complexity of issues that arise in the parish ministry. Things that go wrong, even in small ways, tend to upset and deeply hurt us. Most of us keep a stiff upper lip but the grinding feelings that result from difficult pastor/church member relationships and things that do not go as we had expected or hoped, can lead to more serious troubles down the road. At the very least, they can create one very exhausted and disappointed pastor. When we get in this state of mind, it is too easy to miss the myriads of little wonderful things that go on every day in our ministerial lives.

Pastors get discouraged. They seldom have someone they can easily and appropriately turn to when they've been giving their all

INTRODUCTION

to their people, but things are still not going smoothly. Sometimes there will be a family member willing to listen to the frustrations, but then the touchy issue of confidentiality arises. Pastors simply cannot complain to another person about any negative feelings related to church members. As they say of Las Vegas, "What goes on in the church office stays in the church office!" And that means the negative feelings are likely to go directly into you, the pastor, and remain in your heart, causing suffering for years if issues are not resolved. You've seen those pastors whose smiles are intact but whose eyes are somehow glazed over. This is most often the result of years and years of coping with conflict, with holding back feelings of anger, and with a quiet sense of discouraged acceptance that lingers and grows.

Some pastors even get so discouraged that they seriously consider and, sometimes, do leave the ministry. They dream of setting out to find any kind of life and work in what they see as the "real" world. It is sad to say, but too many good pastors do flee the ministry simply because they feel they have no place to turn to share their feelings. Yet, deep within their hearts and souls, they understand that their call has been set by God, and they know the parish ministry is where they belong. No pastor, however, wants to be unhappy in this calling.[1] Pastors understand their work to be valuable and worthy, even though it often seems impossible.

Throughout the Bible, both God and Christ are described as the "Rock." We think of the Almighty this way in the beautiful old hymn "Rock of Ages cleft for me. Let me hide myself in Thee." We in the parish ministry try our best to always be steady and surefooted. We want to be a rock for our congregations, to be strong for them. But it is far too easy to get discouraged, to secretly blame others, to blame God and, especially, to blame ourselves. Because of this, many good pastors enjoy their work much less than they had hoped and dreamed in their seminary days.

---

1. If you are finding that your sadness or worries are overwhelming, there is help. More will be said about this in an addendum at the conclusion of this book.

INTRODUCTION

Throughout this book, we will address reasons why it is not easy to be a rock in a hard place. But, more importantly, here you will find a safe place to explore your experiences and think of ways of dealing with your feelings about them, leading to avenues toward a deeper spiritual life. With these issues squarely considered and prayed about, you can face your pastoral issues with honesty and grace.

The purpose of this book is to offer some ways for those of us who are pastors to better identify, understand, and maybe even deal with some of the issues that arise in the course of our work, some reasons for that occasional strange behavior of church members toward each other and, too often, toward us, their pastor whom we had hoped they would love. It is intended to offer a bit of perspective on the annoying or, sometimes, even deeply hurtful events of the ministry. It also addresses pastor's honest reactions and offers some ways we might choose to think and pray about them.

PRESENTING THE ISSUE

Each chapter will begin by addressing a specific difficult issue that arises in ordained ministry. Thoughts will be presented that, hopefully, will help the reader to connect his or her own similar or related ministry issue with the topic presented. The purpose is to help us start thinking about the matter. How serious is it? Have we been experiencing anything similar to this if not exactly like it? Have we taken the time to really think about this issue in relation to our ministry in general? Have we thought about how it is affecting us and our ministry?

THE SCENARIO

The scenarios serve to provide short (fictional) stories as examples that demonstrate the issues that are being addressed. Whatever happens to the pastors in these stories is unlikely to be exactly what is happening or has happened to you, but any or all the stories might serve to awaken any thoughts or feelings you have maybe not addressed up until now.

THE THEOLOGICAL REFLECTION

Following each scenario, a short biblical text and reflection will be offered. Each text has been chosen for its relevance to the issue being discussed in the chapter. This gives the reader a chance to consider how certain biblical characters, or sometimes even Jesus himself handled similar difficult human situations.

THE PRAYER

How and what we pray is, of course, a very personal matter. Certainly, you will want to pray in your own words and not necessarily these that are included here. Still, it is hoped that these contemporary prayers will open the reader up to spaces and places where we can meet with the Divine One in relation to each specific issue. Even though we are pastors who pray freely and often, it is less easy to find words when the issues are those that have been hurting us deeply or that have made us feel out of control or embarrassed or less on top of things.

On the other hand, there may be some situations in which you really do want to pray these prayers as they are presented or use some parts of them for your own time with God. These prayers are written in contemporary language and are intended to go directly to the heart of the issue, our own pain, and the related feelings. They are meant to help us know we are not alone and to give us strength for the work ahead.

BOOK IN THREE SECTIONS

The book is divided into three sections. The first deals with situations and issues that bring about specific negative personal feelings

INTRODUCTION

on the part of the pastor. The second section addresses some specific problems that arise in almost every ministry. The third offers discussion regarding the choices we make, as well as possible actions and their very real consequences. This book does not try to solve ministerial problems, because each is unique to a particular congregation and its pastor. And, of course, it is also not good to simply moan over our discomfort. But the book will show you that, as a pastor who has these matters to deal with, you are not alone. We try not to be lone wolves, but the truth is we tend to do much of our stewing over these issues in solitary, often thinking that if we speak about them we will be seen as a bad pastor. It is hoped that just reading about the suffering we share will open us to finding solutions for ourselves and our congregations, and that it will also heal our discomfort, so we can really begin to love our work.

THEOLOGICAL REFLECTION ON BEING CALLED

> Then I heard the voice of the Lord saying, "Whom shall I send, and who will go for us?" And I said, "Here, I am; send me!" (Isa 6:8)

As pastors well know, there are any number of books and reflections written over the years on the topic of what it means to be called into God's service. Of course, that service might not always be to ordained ministry, as those who teach, work with children, work in hospitals, as well as singers and other musicians also work for the same "boss."

Recognizing that you as a pastor are aware of the implications of being called to ordained ministry, let's take a few minutes to have a second look at the well-traveled passage of Isa 6. We who are called rarely miss the point of the writer's confession to being "a man [person] of unclean lips and I live among a people of unclean lips" (Isa 6:5). We probably have not convinced ourselves that we are without sin or without imperfections. We know too that God is liable to call just about anyone and there is no accounting for God's choices. Moses had murdered an Egyptian. Paul had been the hated Saul of Tarsus who persecuted Christians. And we are well aware that it is from such a list of sometimes unsure and often far from perfect human beings that we have come. But what we might miss in this powerful passage from Isaiah is that God actually asks him "Whom shall I send?" And it is Isaiah himself who makes the choice to do it when he answers, "Send me" (or as I once heard in a recitation of this passage many years ago, maybe spoken softly with a timid unbelieving voice, "Send me?" Surely, we could not be the only ones God had to choose from. Yet we've heard God ask, in some way of our own that no other person could probably really understand, "Whom shall I send?" And we have responded.

That means our calling is set from that moment. Each of us has had a different experience of calling and each also has a very different experience of ministry. Yet, I expect that many if not all the situations and scenarios this book offers will ring true to some extent in your own ministry. We are not naïve about our calling. Nobody ever said it would be easy but, on the other hand, so little of what we experience is like what we learned in seminary. But calling is not just about being chosen. It is even more about being chosen to be faithful. You are faithful or you would not have picked up this book. You may have felt reluctant until now to give any deep thought to the negative issues of your ministry. So, let it be said, as we are still at the outset of this journey, that this book is to help you to spend positive time in relation to the issues you struggle with, offering an outlet for your feelings so you can begin to direct yourself to options and maybe even solutions. God chose you, and you said, "Send me." That is the most important thing to remember.

SECTION ONE
Feelings

CHAPTER ONE.
Called to a (not so) perfect congregation

THE ISSUE

Who of us serves a perfect congregation? There is, of course, no such thing. However ideal they may seem from the outside to the committee that chose you as pastor, or to you when you first arrived, they, like any other group of people, consist of the good and the less good, the arrogant, the over-emotional, the sick and weary, the troubled, and all the rest. We are Christians and, according to Paul, also saints. Still, it was Martin Luther who proclaimed that all parishes are filled with both saints and sinners and that the true church is known by God alone. Some pastors today even go so far as to say a church is a hospital. If people were perfect, they would not have a reason to come to church. They are seeking healing and wholeness. This is not to say that any individual person is only sinner or only saint. Most are both, as every pastor knows.

Some congregations are more difficult than others, but few are without any conflict. Many of the troubles within a church are carefully hidden. Some conflict is among members. Some is old conflict that has been swept under the rug for generations and is hard to detect. Some conflict comes up between individuals or groups against the pastor. As their pastor, you dearly want to love them, and you hope they will love or at least respect you. You try your best, but loving them and understanding them is not always the same issue. Even if you have a delightful congregation, there are still nearly always one or two difficult church members. Whatever party might be responsible for any existing disagreements, you and your people are bound together in Christ's love and in mutual responsibility for the mutual upbuilding of the reign of God. These difficulties may or may not be resolved. Resolution is not the intention of this book. The book is, rather, for you the pastor—to be able to take an honest look at these issues, and to guide you into ways you personally can deal with the day-to-day challenges and know you are fulfilling your calling with faithfulness and honor.

SCENARIO

Pastor Janet had always dreamed of being a pastor. The church, she hoped, would be like the one she'd grown up in. That church, in her memories of home, was a place of love and warmth. She'd always felt welcome there and loved. The old people had always smiled at her and supported her youthful plans and dreams. The pastor was friendly and wise. The choir, in her memories, had always sung sweetly. Maybe her old home church was the very reason she'd chosen to be a pastor.

What happened that things should be so difficult now? How did she find herself in a church so different from the one she had loved? She knew what she was getting into. She'd been called now to serve a troubled church. Smith Street Church was losing its members. The congregation had gone over its budget and not met its financial burdens now for almost five years. Janet wondered why she had been chosen to try to solve these problems, and she was not so sure she knew where to begin. To add to her problems, the people in this church bore little resemblance to the sweet folks of her home church. Too often she found them to be unkind to each other, and sometimes also to her. This church had a long history, and the neighborhood had changed. Maybe it was time for the congregation to change as well. Janet had a huge job ahead of her, a job that could only be accomplished with the full support of these people she served and the help of God.

Pastor Janet did not feel prepared for this. She sensed that she didn't have the courage or the ability to do all that had to be done. At this early stage in her ministry, she knew one thing. These people and this church were definitely not what she had dreamed about. But she also knew that through God, all things were possible. She'd stop dreaming about her past life and her ideal church. She would roll up sleeves, do a lot of praying, get to know these people better, and together they were going to make it work!

THEOLOGICAL REFLECTION

> By the rivers of Babylon—there we sat down and there we wept when we remembered Zion. (Ps 137:1)

This passage is one of lament and describes the people of Israel in exile in Babylon. But the words also describe the feeling of deep sorrow experienced by any person who is in a painful place now, while sadly remembering a happier time or place.

We must never forget the joys we experienced in the past, and they can help us get through the worst of times. But, we have also to face the reality of the situation we are in right now. The Bible shows us how the Jewish people adapted to and even contributed to the society they lived in while never forgetting who they were and whose they were. The pain of what is good that is lost can be used to give us direction as we move toward a better future for ourselves and for the people we serve.

PRAYER

God, great and wonderful God, you know I care for my congregation. I have to admit that in so many ways I love them. Still, as well you know, they are far from perfect. They are seldom if ever willing to admit that they have any faults. Most of the time they don't seem to understand what I am trying to do for them and with them. I pour out so much of my love, concern, and hard work. In return I find that I am mistrusted, doubted, and sometimes even treated like the enemy.

I want to ask you this question, God. Is it really me they are so angry with, or do you think maybe it's you? Could it be that they need to raise their voices at me because they don't know they are allowed to do the same to you!

My people may not know how Abraham argued with you trying to convince you not to destroy the city. They may not remember how Job railed against you with all his being, demanding that you be a just God as you had promised. Help me, O God, to be their teacher as well as their leader.

Maybe, on the other hand, they want to hurt me because someone or something is hurting them. Help me to remember that I might be the only person in their lives that they believe is safe to fight with. Open my mind and heart to realize that I do not know and probably will never know their real story, their whole story. They probably don't even know why they treat me this way. Help them to understand themselves. And help me to understand myself.

Give me patience with them, O God. Help me to realize that nobody is perfect, least of all me. Guide me in your paths of peace so that I may serve them with all my heart, with my energy and enthusiasm. They may not be perfect. They are certainly not the ideal congregation to match my particular ministerial skills, as well you know. But, God, you have placed them in my care. You have put us together for this time and in this place for your own reasons. It is our responsibility and our work together to care for each other and to serve you. Help them, O God, and help me.

AMEN

CHAPTER TWO.
Called but feeling annoyed

THE ISSUE

A lot of the time, we are not exactly upset or angry but, rather, we have an ongoing and building sense of annoyance with some (or many) of the people we serve as pastors. It's not easy to care for and preach to people who are getting on our nerves. Blaming ourselves, at least at the beginning, is probably not a bad idea. We can ask ourselves why we think we are feeling this way. It could possibly be our fault. If we're guilty, we can work on changing, forgiving ourselves, forgiving them, and getting on with it. If, upon careful examination of the situation, we discover we are indeed innocent victims of other people's behavior, then we can deal with that in the best ways we know.

One reason our church members upset us so easily is that, as pastors, we are expected to always be "nice." There are many situations in which we cannot simply tell the person what we think. Some may find it dishonest not to go straight to the person, persons, or group who are causing our discomfort, but that isn't always appropriate. The reason is related to power. We may feel particularly powerless in this kind of situation. In fact, as a pastor, we nearly always have a good deal of power to hurt people's feelings deeply. Often the very ones who are giving us a hard time are people playing power games with us to see how we'll react. Even so, they may be hurt by things we say or do. Many hold their pastor on a pedestal, and often these are the people you least expect. To some extent, you need to try not to hurt them. Still, it isn't easy a lot of the time.

SCENARIO

Pastor Larry had no major complaint with his church's board of trustees. After all, they kept the place afloat, and that meant they kept his paycheck coming. The fact was he was annoyed; well, to be honest, deeply annoyed. When he brought up to the trustees the topic that it was the job of the church council (and not just themselves) to vote and agree upon all major decisions for the church, the trustees had said they agreed with him. Larry had explained to them that this is the way most churches do it. But, to his disappointment, after six months had passed, the trustees continued to hold sway, making most of the decisions simply because they held the purse strings. The problem might have been that they'd been in power so long they probably didn't even realize they were doing it. Or, on the other hand, it may have been that they'd decided to just say "yes" to Larry's suggestion and then carry on as usual. Larry had some decisions to make. He could wait until some major issue came up and then point out to them what they were doing wrong. Or he could bring the topic up yet again at the next trustee's meeting. Another option would be for Larry to go to the church council and let them take the bull by the horns and face down the trustees.

Larry found himself becoming more and more annoyed, and, as the days went by, he realized he was beginning to be annoyed not only at the board of trustees as a group, but at its members as individuals. He started thinking of them more as power mongers and less as church members for whom he'd been called to teach and preach. He started to feel sorry for himself. Was he powerless to change things? Maybe it was entirely his fault. His confidence waned over a period of months as nothing changed. He needed to think more objectively, and he needed to clear his head on the matter. Only then could he be useful in the situation.

THEOLOGICAL REFLECTION

> The Pharisees and Sadducees came, and to test Jesus, they asked him to show them a sign from heaven. He answered them, "When it is evening, you say, 'It will be fair weather, for the sky is red.' And in the morning 'It will be stormy today, for the sky is red and threatening.' You know how to interpret the appearance of the sky, but you cannot interpret the signs of the times. An evil and adulterous generation asks for a sign, but no sign will be given to it except the sign of Jonah." Then he left them and went away. (Matt 16:1–4)

If it tells us anything, this passage reminds us that even Jesus can get annoyed! We all know we ought to keep our tempers at bay and that it's best to be patient with our people, but oh how annoying things can get at times! In this Matthew passage, Jesus gives his critics a terrific answer, knowing that they are only trying to goad him. But it is what he does next that we need to hear. "Then he left them and went away" (v. 4b). This is not, of course, to suggest that you go off angry, but only that there are times, if annoyance is beginning to build up to anger, or if you know you're on the verge of saying something you'll regret, that the best thing is to make a quiet and gracious exit.

PRAYER

Tender, kind, and understanding God, this may not be the best time to come to you in prayer. I am so very annoyed with both my people and myself. It's not so much that I'm bothered by my work, or by the church, but rather I'd say it's the little things. I guess you could say I am agitated. There is a gritty feeling in the pit of my stomach that won't go away.

You, O God, have infinite patience. Still, I know the Bible speaks of times you are very frustrated with us. Your people, after all, have disappointed you for thousands of years. So, then, who am I to complain about the irritations my people cause me? But it is very real, this feeling I have. I worry that it could, in time, affect my calling. When I first wanted to be a pastor, I was so excited about the work I would do for you and for your beloved people. When going to seminary, I was thrilled with the studies and the hopes for the future. When I was new at my work for the church, I felt you so close to me, O God. Now, I sometimes even forget to pray.

Was it arrogant to hope that they would respect me? Was it needy of me to expect that they could love me? God, help me to understand them better and love them even when they are cold.

Help me now O gracious, wonderful God. Help me to find peace inside myself and the ability to cope calmly with the people of my church. Give me patience to know they will move at their own pace, and you will move in yours.

I pray from my heart and in the name of Jesus.
AMEN

CHAPTER THREE.
Called but feeling angry

THE ISSUE

There are doubtless going to be times that we pastors feel much more than annoyed. We can get genuinely angry with one or even many of our people. We are well aware, of course, of how inappropriate that can be. And the last thing in the world we want is that our congregation should come to find out how we feel. Pastors are unrealistically expected by many to be gentle and ever-forgiving, and to never even experience anger. We also know, beneath our sense of anger, that in most cases we likely will have forgiven them and moved on as time passes and difficulties are resolved. Still, our anger at the time is very real, sometimes justified, and needs to be acknowledged. Good pastors must know how to deal with these strong feelings. At some point in their ministry, no doubt, anger will happen.

SCENARIO

Pastor Ray was beyond anger. He was furious. He'd given his associate, Lonnie, every opportunity to do good ministry. He'd afforded Lonnie genuine respect and had lifted him up before the congregation, supporting Lonnie's ideas and plans, and standing with him in whatever ways seemed appropriate and helpful. In his own opinion, he had been a friend to him. Now, he discovered,

Lonnie, after two years at the church, was gathering a group of followers out of the congregation, to undermine Pastor Ray, who was the senior pastor. Pastor Ray had heartily approved the search committee's choice of Lonnie for associate. Lonnie had seemed personable and had the experience and qualifications that seemed to make it a perfect match, maybe even a dream team! Ray had also looked forward to working with another pastor and not having to be the "lone wolf," as they call so many pastors. Ray had hoped for many happy years of shared ministry with Lonnie. Now he was so deeply hurt he could not express it even to his family. But, more than that, he was seething with a cold, white anger that would not go away.

Ray knew his deep sense of anger was not going to pass any time soon, so he decided to try to use it for good. He directed his feelings toward solving the problems Lonnie had created. It was not easy to go and speak with those people that Lonnie had turned against him, but he did. He managed to slow and then stop the surge that had been building up toward getting Lonnie to take over Ray's position. But, once he calmed down, Ray managed to make it work. Eventually, it was not Ray but Lonnie who had to go. Much of Ray's anger departed when Lonnie finally left the church. In time, Ray also forgave those church members who had gone against him to support Lonnie's plan. "I must be a pretty good pastor," Ray thought to himself. "They never even knew how really angry I felt throughout this whole mess." Anger can often be directed for good, but it can also be a very dangerous emotion. Ray was lucky that his anger had not destroyed him.

THEOLOGICAL REFLECTION

> As soon as he came near the camp and saw the calf and the dancing, Moses's anger burned hot, and he threw the tablets from his hands and broke them at the foot of the mountain. He took the calf they had made, burned it with fire, ground it to powder . . . (Exod 32:19–20)

Moses had put his life in jeopardy to lead the people out of the hands of Pharaoh. Now, he has gone up the mountain to meet with Almighty God, a very dangerous business. The least the people could do was pray for him while he was gone and behave. Instead, they made the bad choice to build and then even bow down to and worship a golden calf. Was Moses surprised? Probably! Was he incredibly angry? For sure! And, he had the right to be. He had rescued them from slavery. He had found them food and water. He had been leading them through the desert on their way to the promised land. He had given them his all. And they had blatantly violated his trust.

There is no doubt there will be times in your ministry when you have good reason to be furious. We pastors are expected to be above anger, and to be gentle and forgiving at all times. When all the people around us are losing their tempers, it is our responsibility to keep a cool head and bring the others to a place of peace and reconciliation. All this may be true but, if we are unable to admit our deep feelings and unwilling to openly address them, then they will settle inside us and be harmful to our bodies, our souls, and our ministry.

PRAYER

God, I am just so mad. I can't use the words I'd like to use, but I've got to admit, they've all come to mind. I am so angry with what is happening that I feel out of control. I am supposed to be their leader, and they won't let me lead them. Why did they call me to be their pastor if they didn't want to let me do it? It's not like I'm not a team player. Still, it seems as if they respect anybody's opinion more than they do mine.

I blame myself a lot of the time, yet I sense strongly that much of what goes wrong is not my fault. God, should I be blaming myself? Does it even matter to them whether I do or not? Does it matter to you, God, whose fault it is?

Help me to focus on the task at hand. Help me to calm down enough to see more clearly. Help me to forgive myself for my feelings of anger. And, of course, help me to forgive my people who are hurting themselves and me. Give me grace to understand them and myself better. Calm me, Lord. Calm me down. Give me your strength.

In Jesus' name I ask it—yes, in the name of Jesus who got angry sometimes too.

AMEN

CHAPTER FOUR.
Called but feeling overworked

THE ISSUE

There are still people out there who think pastors have the world's easiest job, actually believing that they work one hour a week—the worship service time on Sunday morning. As you know, nothing could be further from the truth, and most pastors put in a minimum of fifty to sixty hours a week. In addition, their supposed time off is regularly interrupted with phone calls. Today's pastors have cell phones and therefore can be reached pretty much any time. And, they have the additional burden of being expected to respond in a timely manner to emails—sometimes adding up to inordinate numbers of hours in a given day. Pastors strive for one day a week off, when most everyone else needs and gets two days. When people are ill or have any kind of emergency, the pastor drops everything in his or her own life and hastens to their side. No problem. After all, we are called to care. Still, people tend to expect the pastor to go through every crisis that they're having, which leaves little time for the pastor's own crises! In pastoral care courses, seminarians are warned that they can be more helpful to their people if they are able to remain calm and stay relatively objective, but this can be perceived by some as lack of concern. Pastors are blamed for just about everything that can go wrong at the church, from a dripping faucet to a decrease in the membership roster. If you're a pastor who can handle all this pressure without feeling overworked, you might want to write a book for everyone else!

There are, in fact, books by the dozen that will tell you that you must take care of yourself. But few, if any, really offer a practical method to make that self-care happen. How can we manage self-care when there's no time left for it? What price might we have to pay for the things that don't get done when we do choose time for some self-care? On the other hand, what will happen if we don't take care of ourselves?

SCENARIO

It's not that George was trying to be super-pastor, not at all. He just wanted to be faithful and relatively efficient and possibly get a bit of respect in the process. But, as it was going these days in the church he served, he could rarely even seem to catch up. There was the paperwork he had to send in regularly to his denominational offices, the confirmation class, and the endless round of evening committee meetings that everyone expected him to attend. On top of it, only he had the huge responsibility to come up with an excellent weekly sermon. (Those Sundays came around with lightening speed! George had always intended to get a week or two ahead on them, but that was just not happening.) Then there were the youth group events, special dinners, and the seemingly endless counseling sessions with individuals. Sometimes he wished he'd not "billed" himself as good at counseling when interviewing for the position. It meant he was getting a lot of calls from church members who, to be honest, he thought might well have worked their problems out on their own if they hadn't thought they had a resident expert, free of charge, at the church. George knew that right now was the time to make some decisions. He would either have to lessen his counseling responsibilities or admit to his congregation that he was overwhelmed. He didn't want to disappoint them when they'd put so much trust in him.

George took a long time to realize that he needed to get away for a bit and try to make some decisions about what the priorities should be for his ministry. He couldn't see the forest for the trees. He could go on like this and do everything they expected of him in a mediocre way or choose what was important and then simply tell them this was the way it was going to be. Knowing this was the first step! Once George got a bit of rest, he began to see what tasks he could do best, and which ones could be given to others. He set out a plan for priorities and started to teach church members to sincerely respect his off-hours. It didn't always work perfectly, but George soon felt much better because he had more control. Yes, he even started to see himself as a better pastor.

THEOLOGICAL REFLECTION

> Now during those days he [Jesus] went out to the mountain to pray, and he spent the night in prayer to God. And when day came, he called his disciples and chose twelve of them. (Luke 6:12–13a)

Jesus is an excellent role model for us pastors. When he has decisions to make or matters to ponder about, we read that he goes away for a time alone to pray. We don't get details or exact words he may have spoken to his beloved "Father," but we understand the message for any individual or community that reads the text. If Jesus needs time away from the fray, certainly we do as well. Too often, we pastors think we have to be "on the job" in one way or another for twenty-four hours a day. Everyone will tell us we need to take time to pray, but we also need time that's simply away from the everyday grind of trying to fulfill everyone's needs and be true to our calling.

PRAYER

God, I have felt so tired for so long. I'm entirely exhausted. I admit to you that I've blamed our people for the way I feel. Maybe it is their fault, and maybe it's mine, for not taking care of myself. But, instead of blaming anyone, help me to know that your will for all of us is that we do find rest.

I pray for my people, O God. Make them sufficient to the tasks you call them to do. Help them to be strong. And, as their pastor, O God, give me the courage to do my work faithfully, and the wisdom to know when and how to share that work with them and to slow down. Help me to truly take care of myself so that I can be strong for them.

When I sleep, may my sleep be full and restful. When I eat, may the food nourish and strengthen me to your service. When I work, may I do it with all of my heart. And, when I pray, may I always feel your loving warmth surrounding me and bringing peace. I ask all these things, O Great One, also for my people. May all that we do in your name be worthy of your love.

I ask this in the name of Jesus who worked tirelessly but also knew when to go away for a while and rest.

AMEN

CHAPTER FIVE.
Called but feeling confused

THE ISSUE

We who are pastors generally feel pretty good about our education. Yet there are times when we are not totally in control of situations. Parish ministry is so varied and complex, even in the smallest church family. We are sometimes confused. It is usually not long before things straighten themselves out. In the meantime, we can feel pretty stupid. How can it be that we are not on top of things? Why is it that we don't have all the information we need to make informed decisions? How did this particular issue get out of our control? We rarely have anyone to confide in about any sense of confusion we may be having, because nobody wants a pastor who is not on top of things and in control of both the big picture and all the small details.

But the fact is that people may not really need their pastor to be in the know about everything. It's often our own perception of what is expected of us that gives us the feeling we have to be in charge all the time.

SCENARIO

Ever since she was a young adult, Pastor Linda had prided herself in being in control and in knowing what was going on around her.

Raised without siblings, she had often felt left out as a child and became too easily unnerved when other young people seemed to be in the know and she was not included in games and activities. Now Linda had matured. She was a young pastor, educated and respected. How then could she have allowed things to get out of her control like this? She was confused.

Not too many pastors had to go through what Linda and her congregation had faced. There had been a terrible fire in the church. The sanctuary of their historic building was pretty much gutted. The insurance money was substantial. Importantly, no one was in the building at the time of the fire. The reason for Linda's terrible confusion was this. One group in the church, led by a rather powerful long-time trustee, had the idea that they should use the money to build a new church in a different part of town. His argument was that the downtown neighborhood had seen its day and that they should rebuild elsewhere because the current location offered the congregation no future. In the meantime, a second equally strong group had formed. That second group consisted of those who felt very strongly that they needed to stay where they were. They felt that, if the neighborhood was indeed failing, then that was even more reason for the historic congregation to stand its ground, right there. Many of these people had either been born into this congregation, or had perhaps married there, or had children baptized and raised there. They had roots in the place. For them, the building itself was beloved. Yes, it had suffered a fire, but now it could be made beautiful again. Both groups were zealous.

Now Pastor Linda found herself in the middle of the controversy. She was confused because, try as she may, pray as she would, and analyze as she did, she could not figure out how one of these groups was right and the other wrong. Both groups were gathering momentum and asking (or more demanding) her total support! What a dilemma she was in. Shouldn't she have a strong opinion? If she did, then what would happen to the group of the opposite persuasion? How would they come to feel about their pastor? Would they even leave the church? It was worrying. The more Linda tried to think about what to do, the more confused she became. It occurred to her that both she and her congregation were suffering from some kind of post-fire syndrome! A devastating fire in one's place of worship is a deeply felt event, and the people's very strong opinions as to how they should respond to this tragedy were very likely related to their suffering over the loss of this place of prayer they loved so deeply.

In time, Linda's confusion turned to resolution and then to action. After much prayer and consideration, and after trying to talk with everyone, she determined that it was more important for her to be ministering to their deep emotional and spiritual needs and less to necessarily agree with their early plans. She arranged a series of public prayers and thanksgiving services, to take place in neighboring worship spaces but led by her people. At these, although she did not tell them their decisions were less than important, she chose to focus on the fact that to live in this world means we have to live with change. She preached about how God is doing a new thing. And she threw herself into serving their needs instead of appeasing their demands. To her surprise, the people began to rally, and it was not long before they began to come together with their ideas about how to proceed. As it turned out, the congregation decided to stay at the old location and rebuild the interior, maintaining the historic stone edifice. As years passed, they were glad they had committed to staying in the downtown area.

THEOLOGICAL REFLECTION

> The woman said to the serpent, "We may eat of the fruit of the trees in the garden; but God said, 'You shall not eat of the fruit of the tree that is in the middle of the garden, nor shall you touch it, or you shall die.'" But the serpent said to the woman, "You will not die, for God knows that when you eat of it your eyes will be opened, and you will be like God, knowing good and evil." So, when the woman saw that the tree was good for food and that it was a delight for the eyes and that the tree was to be desired to make one wise, she took of its fruit and ate,

and she also gave some to her husband, who was with her, and he ate. (Gen 3:2–6)

Eve was confused! God had made clear that they were not to eat the fruit of this particular tree. But now this smart talking serpent had been saying the opposite. He seemed so wise, so logical, and his words fed into Eve's curiosity. Now she was thinking about having a taste after all. As the story goes, she not only went ahead and ate of the fruit forbidden by God, but she also gave some to her husband who gobbled it up for whatever reason. He seems to have been confused as well, because we don't know for sure if he ate it because he wanted the "knowledge of good and evil" that it promised, or because he was obeying his wife, or simply because he was hungry! Well, we all know the rest of the story. Because of Eve's confusion, everything changed! Clarity is so important, in times of temptation, and also in times of difficulty. Still we often get confused about things and, for us too, it can cause a good deal of trouble.

The good news here is that, even though God told them if they ate the fruit they would surely die, God did not choose to kill them! They got themselves into a big mess and there would be unimaginable consequences, but Adam and Eve did not die. We will very likely have times in our ministerial leadership when we too are confused. It is good to remember that, however misguided our decisions may be and however confused we may become, God is for us, and not against us.

PRAYER

O Creator of the Universe, it was you who took chaos and confusion and created from them a world of beauty and order. You understand all our human feelings. Help me to move away from this sense of confusion that I am experiencing at this time. You know, O God, that most of the time I know well what I am doing in my life, and I am even able to help others. I generally consider myself a useful person. I have always taken pride in being in control.

CALLED BUT FEELING CONFUSED

Perhaps I have been too prideful. Forgive me God, if this is so. Either way, I do confess that, as this time, I am confused, and I don't like it.

I worry that the people of the church I serve will notice my confusion. It is difficult to hide these feelings, and I am the person responsible for leading the community. Give me direction. Give me your wisdom. Clear away the foggy feelings.

Order my life in your favor and direct my work in ways that are best for all concerned. Help me to find a clear direction and a strong peace of mind.

Even your greatest leaders were confused at times. David was a great leader and powerful king, but he didn't always have a clear vision and seemed often to be confused about things. Still, he always opened himself up to your leading, he listened to the wisdom of your prophets, he received your blessing, and, in time, David found his way. Great God, may I be willing to do the same. When I am confused like this, O God, give me clarity. Give me direction. Give me a strong sense of your ongoing and unending presence.

I pray all this in the name of Jesus, in the knowledge that, if I try my best to follow his teachings and his leadership, and if I always remember his love for me, then, in your good time, my confusion will pass away.

AMEN

CHAPTER SIX.
Called but feeling disjointed

THE ISSUE

People expect the pastor to be on top of things all the time. When parishioners are upset with us or rude or unreasonable, we are expected to turn the other cheek. In addition, too many people expect us to be all things to all people! And, of course, we cannot. There are times when our busy schedules and too many demands can cause us to feel disjointed.

SCENARIO

There wasn't really anything wrong. The church was moving along and growing at a reasonable rate. The church members seemed to be happy. At least, Pastor Jason hadn't heard any complaints. He'd been with them for seven years now. He hadn't had a raise for some time, but that could be expected in these difficult times. What, if anything, could be bothering him that made him feel so disjointed, so different from the way he had felt up till now?

Jason tried to get to the bottom of it. He decided to go through his day-to-day activities and compare them to those he had listed in his calendar from one year back, two years back, and five years back. The results were quite a surprise to him. It seems his activities had changed quite drastically in recent months compared to what he had been doing back then. Right up until this year, Jason had spent more time in prayer, more time with his family, and more time in study of Scripture and related readings. Once he saw all this in writing, he figured out what had been making him feel so disjointed. His giving of himself to others, which is of course a very good thing, had built up to more and more hours. His taking time to strengthen his own faith and increase his own knowledge, as well as his precious time with family, had diminished little by little. It was clearly time to get back in balance! Jason felt relieved just thinking about it.

THEOLOGICAL REFLECTION

> From there he [Jesus] set out and went away to the region of Tyre. He entered a house and did not want anyone to know he was there. Yet he could not escape notice, but a woman whose little daughter had an unclean spirit immediately heard about him, and she came and bowed down at his feet. Now the woman was a Gentile, of Syrophoenician origin. She begged him to cast the demon out of her daughter. He said to her, "Let the children be fed first, for it is not fair to take the children's food and throw it to the dogs." But she answered him, "Sir, even the dogs under the table eat the children's crumbs." Then he said to her, "For saying that, you may go—the demon has left your daughter." And when she went home, she found the child lying on the bed, and the demon gone. (Mark 7:24–30)

As pastors, you have very likely preached more than once on this Jesus story. There are many aspects to consider. But the one that seems to jump out at us is that Jesus' first answer to the woman is not classic Jesus. It seems unkind and ill considered. It is only after the woman's brilliant and provocative comeback that Jesus offers to help her.

We tend to always see Jesus as totally in control. This is one story where he seems less so, at least at the beginning. It appears he is trying to get away for a while and not have to give all his attention to the duties of teaching and healing. He seems to need rest. When he doesn't get it, his response to the woman is short and seems almost cruel. It's as if he is saying, "I'm not here for the likes of you." The issue is resolved when the heretofore powerless woman has the courage to confront Jesus, whom she perceives as the one who can solve her problem.

When we're feeling disjointed, we may not be able to solve our own problems. But it is possible that, as in this story of Jesus, communicating with others, sometimes those who are the least likely to be able to help us, can be the ones who get us back on track.

PRAYER

God, as we all know, you are the one who has everything under control. But I, on the other hand, am only human. I've been trying my best, but I admit that I feel . . . well . . . disjointed. Please help me to understand that this is perfectly normal. Help me to see that I do not have to understand everything all the time.

Help me also to seek out others so that, together, we can deal with issues that arise in the complexity of life. Guide me so that I do not discount those people who may not appear to be the ones who can help me.

You, who made everything, and you who love the world, can never be confused or disjointed. Because of your love, I am assured that, in time, your plans for me will take away this feeling, and all will be well.

I ask all this in the name of Jesus who lived in this crazy human world, and had his troubles, just as the rest of us have.

AMEN

CHAPTER SEVEN.
Called but feeling sad

THE ISSUE

We know we can't be happy all the time, but sometimes we pastors have good reasons to be filled with sorrow. At times, we feel sad for others. At other times, it is our own personal issues that make us unhappy. We are little good to anyone in our ministry if we become truly depressed or get overcome with grief. First, let's look at the sadness we might have in relation to others.

SAD ABOUT OTHER PEOPLE'S PROBLEMS

As pastors, most of us are relatively well trained and experienced in giving pastoral care. This means we know, intellectually at least, that it's best not to get personally involved too deeply with other people's problems, illnesses, and suffering. We are taught that, if we do, we are less able to help them. In addition, such involvement, in time, can really wear us down to the point of not being useful to anyone. All that said, it is easier said than done to remain unattached. We are always going to feel something as we stand beside our precious church members in their times of trial, as we sit at the beds of the dying, and as we listen to the stories of mistakes made, breaking marriages, and the rest. We are going to feel filled with sorrow.

It is important that we do not allow this sadness to permeate us and affect our work in negative ways. We deal with so many more problems than most people. We need to be strong for them and remain as objective as we can, without becoming artificial or cold. This requires a delicate balance.

Scenario

Reverend Josephine had been careful over the years of her ministry. She knew not to get tangled up in people's personal problems to the point where she could not be objective and help them to the best of her ability. But this time, for some reason, she'd fallen right into it. She would not, after all, have entered the parish ministry in the first place if she were not compassionate. She'd been a good pastor to the Andrews family for over five years. She had confirmed the two sons of Marge and George and performed the marriage for their daughter. She had officiated at the funeral when George and the eldest son died that night in a car accident. The other son, according to what Marge told her, was now on drugs and failing his college courses. The mother, Marge, was left alone, as her daughter moved to the West Coast, and Marge was slowly becoming more and more dependent on Pastor Josephine. She would drop in at the church office unannounced, make late evening phone calls to her, and now also required hospital visits, as Marge discovered she had a serious illness. Pastor Josephine was beginning to realize that whatever her plan had been in principle (not to get too close and to remain objective), it was much harder to do in reality! She would have to work at this. She would continue to love Marge as a pastor but try to help her find other people to rely on to meet her many needs. Josephine would not desert this now needy woman. She would continue to help and continue to pray for her and with her. But she also could not let one woman, and one family situation, damage her ability to be fair to the rest of her flock. We must not allow another person's grief to overwhelm us. Josephine was learning this firsthand.

Theological Reflection

> Weeping may linger for the night, but joy comes with the morning. (Ps 30:5b)

There is no shortage of sad situations described throughout the Bible, from the death of Abel at the hand of his own brother in the fourth chapter of Genesis, all the way through the crucifixion of Jesus Christ, betrayed by a beloved disciple. Yet, the overriding message of the Bible is one of hope, renewal, and new life. These words from Ps 30 have brought that sense of hope for tomorrow to readers over the millennia. They remind us that, whatever suffering we are experiencing now, things will improve either in the future or, at the very longest, when we come to be with God for eternity.

Prayer

God of Compassion, my people have so many problems that, at times, they overwhelm me with their sorrow. As each one of them comes to me and shares such deep troubles, I find myself taking every problem to my heart, and I feel it is sometimes more than anyone can bear. It's as if they are hoping or expecting that I can solve these issues. Maybe that isn't true, but for me it certainly feels that way. I mean, why aren't they just taking these problems directly to you, God? I do remind them of this (that you are always there to listen to their hearts), but still I feel somehow responsible for their troubles and the fact that they are not being resolved. Help me, O mighty healer of the world, to realize that I am not the healer. Others are better qualified than I. And the true healer is always you.

Help me to think about ways within this world, and in this community, that my people's problems might be solved or eased. Guide me to a clear mind, so that I can help them find help wherever it is available. Oh God, remind me that I am not a solver of problems but, when possible, a facilitator of solutions, so that I can direct them to those who might help and, most of all, guide them to you.

Make me a good listener, God; a listener and a helper—one who helps my people to a happier life. And should their problems be the kind that cannot really be resolved, give me the strength and courage to guide them closer to you. It is only you that can give us a truly calm and trusting heart in times of grave difficulty. Our faith, our trust, and our dependence on you is ultimately what will help us the most in times of trouble.

I pray all this in the name of Jesus who heals those who suffer, who himself suffered that we may be made whole, and who continues to transform lives.

AMEN

SAD ABOUT ONE'S OWN PROBLEMS

Other times, it is we ourselves who are suffering deep sadness. Most times our sadness is for really good reasons. Perhaps some terrible thing has happened to you: the loss of a loved one, overwhelming worries related to financial crisis, or pressing issues such as having had to relocate too often or having to live too far from aging parents or other beloved family members. As pastors, it is important that we are willing to face our personal troubles. Still, we must keep ourselves calm and controlled enough, if at all possible, to be able to serve our church with reasonable focus, energy, and enthusiasm. Where do we find enthusiasm for our work and our people when we are suffering from deep personal sadness?

We might even consider getting some help, possibly from a professional counselor. (Many pastors avoid professional help in fear of being "found out" and either losing their job or putting a blot on their reputations with their denomination. Be assured there are many ways to seek and find professional help in confidence.) In less serious situations, you may be able, with the help of friends and family, to handle your suffering and carry on with your work. You'll need to have someone you trust that you can talk to about your feelings. Yes, we are leaders, but leaders need help when in greatly difficult personal situations just as much as the next person.

Scenario

Pastor Glen had always felt good about his ministerial work. Now, after fifteen years in the ministry, it was he who needed attention. His spouse, Laura, had just been diagnosed with diabetes. She already had a serious heart condition. Aside from that, they were just not making enough money. Month by month, year by year, the two of them were falling deeper in debt. The house was not worth what they had expected, and they still had a pretty sizable mortgage. So, there was no point in trying to sell and get a smaller place. Glen's church council seemed unlikely to offer a raise soon, as membership was down. That too had bothered him, as he wondered if the decline in numbers might be his fault. In short, Glen was worried and sad. He was worried about his precious wife. He couldn't do enough for her. If he increased his workload at the church to try to build up membership and make his people happier, that time would come right out of the time he needed for his precious Laura. He felt so incredibly down.

To add to his problems, some person had gone to the church council to complain that Pastor Glen's sermons and his attitude were becoming "too negative." The council felt badly about telling him but decided they'd better be honest. The council chair explained to Glen that they'd told the person Glen had a lot on his plate at the moment and that they were sure he wouldn't seem "negative" forever. This made Glen feel worse, as it seemed to him that he was being pushed to resolve his problems faster than humanly possible, or maybe even resign.

In time, Glen realized that one person's complaint didn't mean everything. Still, he appreciated that one person's hurtful honesty had showed him how his own personal worries and suffering had been spreading discomfort among the people he was serving.

Theological Reflection

> While he was at Bethany in the house of Simon the Leper, as he sat at the table, a woman came with an alabaster jar of very costly ointment of nard, and she broke open the jar and poured the ointment on his head. But some were there who said to one another in anger, "Why was the ointment wasted in this way? For this ointment could have been sold for more than three hundred denarii and the money given to the poor." And they scolded her. But Jesus said, "Let her alone; why do you trouble her? She has performed a good service for me." (Mark 14:3–6)

This is such a lovely passage. We know that Jesus is deeply troubled at this time. A woman, a stranger, comes to pour a costly balm upon him, to soothe him. She cannot have known how much trouble lay ahead for him and how short his earthly life will be from this time. Her kindly act toward him is seen in the wrong light by others, but Jesus recognizes it as an act of caring and tells them so. Surely, he is deeply moved by her action. We can see from reading this passage that even Jesus had times when he needed consolation. We can't expect ourselves to always be on top of things. We will have our own times of sadness, mourning, and grief. We hope that, in such troubled times, God will send us a situation to turn things for the better, or a person such as this woman, who came to Jesus, to lighten his burden.

Prayer

God, please be with me while I am feeling so terribly sad. Is this some kind of depression or just a temporary sorrow over losses I am currently experiencing? I don't know for sure, because I am immersed in it, and it seems overwhelming to me.

Be with me as I think of the troubles of my dear ones, of my family that I love so much. When I feel helpless to take away their pain, guide me to ask you for help for them. Help me remember they are always in your tender care.

Called but feeling sad

Help me to remember that my personal feeling of sadness is always temporary. It is part of the human experience. Guide me to ask others for help and to choose the right people for this task. Help me to realize that there are many who sincerely care for me.

Help me to remember that there were many times when Jesus felt sad too. He wept over his friend Lazarus. He wept over the city of Jerusalem. Even he could become discouraged. I think he appreciated it when that woman poured that precious, soothing oil over his head. I pray in memory of her and in his holy name.

AMEN

CHAPTER EIGHT.
Called but feeling like a fool

THE ISSUE

No pastor wants to be seen as a fool or to think that he or she is one. Maybe you've made a mistake or some kind of faux pas. It's almost inevitable, considering the variety of work we do and the numerous kinds of work in which people expect us to be experts. You graduated from a seminary (maybe even the best seminary!), but my guess is that it wasn't long before you realized your actual work as a pastor bears little resemblance to what you had actually been trained for. This gap seems enormous when we start out in ministry even though, in time, we come to see the value of our theological education in relation to the work we do. There are many aspects of our work that we do "by the seat of our pants." It's no wonder we make mistakes sometimes.

So, if you're feeling like a fool right now for whatever reason, ask yourself this question: Am I really to blame? If the answer is yes, do the best you can to make things right and then forgive yourself. You may have been a fool for a moment, but you'll be no long-time fool! Try to fix things up as best you can and then "go forth and be a fool no more." If you really are to blame, you might want to ask yourself if there is some reason you did this thing. You may have been overtired or overworked and need a bit of rest. Or, depending on the severity of the action, it may be time for you to think about getting things right and then possibly even moving on. Chances are, however, that this is not the case. So, don't make any major judgments while you're still feeling like a fool. Wait till the issue passes if you can. Then, your head will be clear for making any major decisions.

If the answer is no, you are not responsible for whatever happened that made you feel or look like a fool, then you have two choices. One: You can direct the blame to the person or persons responsible, which would let you off the hook. (This often won't work in ministry because, as well you know, the pastor can't go around accusing church members even when they are guilty!) Or, two: There's a good chance you may have to take the rap and simply see that this thing never happens again. If this is the case, be consoled by reminding yourself that you are, indeed, not a fool but are just covering for someone as a kindness or gesture of pastoral love.

If you truly have been made to look bad and are not inclined to let it go, it is possible you may have to confront the person who did this thing to you. When you talk to the person truthfully, be sure that you "speak the truth in love." You will know best whether this is a good option, depending on the person who did this thing. Try to keep perspective. There are worse things than being made to feel like a fool. If you know you're not a fool, this uncomfortable feeling will pass in time. If you are a fool, well, you can change!

SCENARIO

Pastor Martha was embarrassed. She had waited way too long to make her final preparations to go out to the cemetery for a particular graveside service. Now, what was happening to her was unbelievable. She had only a half hour left to drive to the cemetery, which was forty minutes away. She grabbed her coat, keys, Bible, and notebook. But she could not anywhere locate the small cardboard container that contained the ashes of the deceased! The gentleman had passed away three months earlier in the coldest part of winter. His family had decided to wait and hold the graveside service when the weather had improved, and today was the day. The way Martha remembered it, the man's brother had the ashes delivered to her office back in winter, and she had tucked them away in the back of a filing cabinet, intending to bring them out today so they could be spread over the ground on the grave of his beloved wife. So, where were the ashes now? In a cold panic, Martha hunted her office. They were not in any drawer. They were not hidden behind the books in her bookcase where she sometimes placed ashes before family came to pick them up. (She didn't want them to be seen by the people coming in and out.) When there was no place left to look, she broke down and called the funeral home. Martha was feeling deep embarrassment and could feel her face was flushing, even though she was alone in her office. A man answered the phone. After identifying herself, Martha spoke up: "I wonder if you could tell me something . . . in confidence. Do you have the ashes of Timothy Holmes there, and are you bringing them with you out to the grave site this afternoon?" The person at the other end could not help himself. His answer began with a firm, "No, we definitely do not have Mr. Holmes's ashes here, nor are they in the car which left ten minutes ago for the grave site." Martha collapsed into her office chair, panic mounting. She'd lost the ashes! She was totally responsible. What would be the consequences of such a terrible mistake? What would the family say? After what seemed too long a pause, the person on the other end of the telephone continued, and now she could hear the amusement in his voice as he spoke. "But you will be happy to know the late Mr. Holmes was never cremated. It's his body in the casket and it's on its way to the grave site and . . . well, you'd better get going or you'll be late." Martha's relief was impossible to describe. She thanked the man with as much courtesy as she could muster, feeling glad she had not been talking to him face to face. She hung up the phone and ran out of the office to her car. The cemetery was not easy to find there in the country, but when she arrived, she located the funeral home people, the gathered family, and, much to her relief, one very fine oak casket containing the remains of Mr. Holmes. All through the short service she led, Martha could still feel profound embarrassment. What a complete fool she'd been. She promised herself she would never ever let a thing like this happen again. She was only able to calm down inside when she realized that the chances of such a thing happening again were highly unlikely. She'd be wiser tomorrow and more experienced for all this having happened. Still, today there was no doubt about it. She was the fool and had no one to blame but herself.

THEOLOGICAL REFLECTION

> Do not deceive yourselves. If you think that you are wise in this age, you should become fools so that you may become wise. For the wisdom of this world is foolishness with God. (1 Cor 3:18–19a)

We may not realize it when it's happening to us, but feeling like a fool, or even being a fool is not the worst thing that could happen. Human wisdom is always faulty, as this passage makes clear. It is only God's wisdom that counts in the end. We may well be fools much of the time.

The work we're doing to build up the reign of God can at times make us seem foolish to people. The wisdom of the world is not the same as the wisdom of God, after all. So often we look foolish when trying to help the poor, lift up those who are troubled, or give ourselves away on what may seem foolish to the rest. As this passage suggests, we may very well even have to be role models of foolishness to guide our congregations in the ways of Christ.

PRAYER

God, I'm pretty sure I've made a bit of a fool of myself. Perhaps I am holding to a standard too high for my human condition. Or maybe my judgments have been less than perfect. I am aware of that. Whatever the truth may be, I know that you know it. Still, right now I feel like a fool.

Being a Rock in a Hard Place

I am well aware that discernment is a gift from you, dear God. Some of us have it by nature more so than others. Still, I do believe I have enough intelligence. Help me to use it. Give me the discernment I need to look objectively at the situation. Then, once I have correctly judged my own behavior in this situation, help me to make the right moves to rectify anything that needs attention. If I need to apologize to someone, give me the courage to do so with sincerity. If I need to forgive someone, help me to do that. If it is only I who need to forgive myself, then let me do that. If I need to start fresh in certain areas of my life, help me to know you will be with me through it all. My mistakes are human mistakes. Please help me to learn from them but also to have the courage to go on.

You, who guided Moses and the people of Israel through the wilderness, guide me through mine.

AMEN

CHAPTER NINE.
Called but feeling like laughing

THE ISSUE

There are times in the parish ministry when we can barely contain ourselves. Situations that have upset and disappointed and hurt us have come to a head, or they have gone on for an inordinate amount of time. We have not been able to solve the problem, raise the money, or (in many cases) please that one constantly perturbed individual church member. The moment comes when all we want to do is laugh. Needless to say, we have to do this kind of laughing in private. It is tempting to want to share our viewpoint or that now seemingly hilarious story with a friend but, in most cases, we are required to keep confidence, so we must say nothing.

Pastors and counselors with long experience in ministry know that people do often laugh inappropriately at times of greatest difficulty or deepest grief. So, it is possible that this may be the reason we feel like laughing. We're not always quick to recognize when we are in grief ourselves. We deal so much with other people's suffering that we do not always see when we're not being objective as we'd like to be. When tending to their needs, although behaving with understanding, we know we can serve them best by staying emotionally uninvolved. Still, we wouldn't have gone into the ministry if we didn't feel deeply for people. Total objectivity is simply impossible. Sometimes the problems of the people we serve come too heavily, one after another, and we are set on an emotional roller coaster. When this happens, it might be good to just go to a movie. Or we can set some time aside to enjoy an evening with friends or family. We might even simply sit down and write about what it is that we are laughing about, and then read it, rip it up, and toss it out.

Still, whatever you do, don't feel bad about the urge to laugh. Please be as patient and understanding with yourself as you would with any of your church people. Remember you are often under much more pressure than you have been willing to admit to yourself. You may need some time off, or you may just feel different in a day or two. More likely, it is simply time to follow your instincts here—have a good hearty laugh and get over it. When you feel like laughing, do just that, but just wait until you are in a place alone!

SCENARIO

Hank had been a pastor for sixteen years. He figured that, till that one day, pretty much everything that could happen to a religious leader had happened to him in one way or another. Hank was what you might call an "old pro," but this latest thing he had not seen coming, and it took him completely by surprise. It happened at the council meeting, after a long, rough day of ministry. He was just sitting there, quietly putting up with a mounting load of the usual complaints from that one church member named Jim. Jim had started up that evening complaining about the fact that by the end of the year they could expect to be way over budget. Then Jim moved on to tell everybody at the meeting how disturbed he was by the worship service going what he called "overtime" for two weeks in a row. Following that, he complained that those teenagers in the back were not paying attention at the service and the pastor should do something about it. It was at this point that the laughter started welling up from deep inside Pastor Hank. Following this diatribe, good old Jim apparently was far from finished. He was also upset about the fact that the church doors that had been painted that week were totally the wrong shade of burgundy. "Looks more like a house of ill-repute" were his exact words. That was the last straw. Anyone could have expected Pastor Hank to get angry or at least be seething inside. Instead, the worst happened. Hank laughed out loud. It was what you might even call raucous! There was a shocked silence. All that Hank could think was "Well, it's been nice working here." This made him laugh even louder. What a disaster. How would he ever get out of this incredible faux pas? Pastors are expected to be serious people. But, as it turned out, Hank was saved! The others at the meeting picked up on Hank's response, and they too started to smile. And that's when some kind of miracle happened. Hank looked over at old complaining Jim, the perennial naysayer and troublemaker, and saw that (miracle of miracles!) Jim was laughing too. "Well, maybe not a house of ill repute," Jim added, "but that color on the doors does indicate a certain lack of dignity. I think I could get a couple of men together to try to get a better mix and we'll just go ahead and paint the doors again. We should be able to get it right this time." By this point, Pastor Hank had regained his composure, and the rest had settled down. Everyone was surprised at the grace with which Jim the troublemaker had taken the pastor's inappropriate response to his comment. And the usually negative Jim himself seemed perfectly okay. It appeared he was just as happy to receive this kind of attention as if he had won all his arguments. Could it be that Jim's life was just lonely, and one kind of attention was just as welcome to him as another? "Well," thought Pastor Hank, "I guess I'm not getting fired after all. It would have been pretty crazy to get fired for laughing. We live and learn."

THEOLOGICAL REFLECTION:

> They [the three men/angels] said to him [Abraham], "Where is your wife Sarah?" And he said, "There, in the tent." Then one said, "I will surely return to you in due season, and your wife Sarah shall have a son." And Sarah was listening at the tent entrance behind him. Now Abraham and Sarah were old, advanced in age; it had ceased

to be with Sarah after the manner of women. So Sarah laughed to herself, saying, "After I have grown old, and my husband is old, shall I be fruitful?" (Gen 18:9–12)

There are not a lot of places in the Bible where people are said to actually laugh, but we find this one example in Genesis. Many serious people might think that Sarah's laughter was entirely inappropriate, not to mention its being a very strange reaction. The text tells us that both she and her husband Abraham are past the age of childbearing. They have no children and, in early Jewish culture, this would have been a source of many years of suffering and embarrassment to them both, but especially to Sarah. Women's prime responsibility in this culture was to bear children to carry on the family name. It is very possible that her laughter was an outlet for her profoundly deep feelings about this issue. We are not told for sure; only that she laughed and later lied about it, saying that she had not.

Another possible reason Sarah laughed is that she was mature enough to see the irony in the situation. All the years when they might have had a child, no angels appeared. Now when the gig is up and the game is over—now they show up and make this seemingly impossible promise! Good timing, angels! Life can take turns that we least expect, and so many things happen at unlikely and inconvenient times. These may well be times to take the hint from Sarah and also be mature. Go into your "tent" when no one is looking and just have a good laugh.

PRAYER

O God who created the world and this entire universe, right now I just want to laugh so hard. Please understand my laughter. It is not these individuals in my church that I'm laughing at, as I'm sure you know. I guess it is the human condition—our vulnerability, our stupidity, our silly mistakes, our incredible selfishness, our lack of concern for your kingdom.

CALLED BUT FEELING LIKE LAUGHING

O God, I know you will understand and forgive my giddiness. I know you alone know that my laughter comes out of my really deeply caring. I care for the people I'm laughing about. I care for the situation we are in. I care about our church and the work we're doing. I know you let me laugh as an outlet. It's because you love me that you let me laugh at all this. Help me to take this sense of lightness and use it as a way toward rest and renewal. May my laughter (and other people's laughter if they too are laughing) build up our strength for the serious work we always have to do, in order to build your reign and help make a better world.[1]

I pray now in Jesus' name.
AMEN

---

1. I remember a drawing I once saw called "Laughing Jesus," and it is my deepest hope that, indeed, Jesus did find time to laugh.

CHAPTER TEN.
Called but feeling betrayed

THE ISSUE

Throughout the Psalms, we read the words of people who have been betrayed or at least felt betrayed by enemies and sometimes even by friends.

In many ways, betrayal is the worst thing that can happen and hurts the most. If we've suffered feelings of betrayal because people in the church have not stood up for us, we are hurt but not damaged. If, on the other hand, we really have been betrayed, then we have good reason to be hurting. The problem is this. How are we going to deal with it so our suffering does not harm our ministry and so we can stop hurting?

SCENARIO

When Pastor Laura came to Oak Road Church, her staunchest supporter was Marianne, the chair of the search committee. In the past three years, she and Marianne had become friends, although she tried to be careful not to show partiality. Still, they had shared meals together, had been on committees for the community outside the church, and had together represented their church as the lay and pastoral members of a committee to attend a national denominational gathering. If there was one person Pastor Laura believed she could trust, it would have been Marianne.

For this reason, she was even more surprised at what Marianne did—or rather what she did not do. Marianne's sister Blanche was also a church member, and Blanche had put together a group to try to remove Pastor Laura. How could it be that Blanche would do such a thing and not let her own sister know about it? Besides, once the proceedings started, Laura was sure she could see in Marianne's eyes that she had known about it all along. Yet, Marianne apparently had stood by and not even tried to stop it. Not only that, but she had given Laura no warning. If she had told her how that group was going to proceed behind her back, she could have done so many things. Laura could have put together some kind of defense against the false accusations. She might at the very least have had heads-up on looking for a new position somewhere else. But, as it turned out, Pastor Laura, who had given her whole self to the work of this congregation, was being maligned and now summarily dismissed by a self-appointed committee of dissidents led by the sister of her best friend! Did Marianne's friendship with her mean nothing? She had heard that blood is thicker than water, but this was more than she could bear. Laura was hurting! She was betrayed.

THEOLOGICAL REFLECTION

> Even my close friend in whom I trusted, who ate of my bread, has lifted the heel against me. (Ps 41:9)

In Ps 41, the writer speaks mainly about enemies in the guise of friends who come to visit him when he is ill. They "utter empty words while their hearts gather mischief" (v. 6). Still, what hurts him the most by far is that his best friend, his friend with whom he shared meals, has also turned against him and has betrayed him. As the psalm proceeds, we can feel the depth of the suffering of betrayal the psalmist experiences. Yet, in the end, what counts is that God is on his/her side. She has the support and love of the Creator and has maintained integrity as well (v. 12). If we can remember that no person can take our integrity from us, then, even though betrayal hurts mightily, we can overcome the pain of it in time.

The Hebrew word for love, *hesed*, has a complex meaning including such things as doing for the other person whatever is required to meet that person's needs without expectation of reward. But the primary aspect of this word for love is nothing less than loyalty. To be loyal is to demonstrate love toward another person.

PRAYER

Great God, I know that many people in the Bible stories experienced feelings of betrayal, and that our own Lord Jesus was betrayed by Judas his friend, leading directly to his death. Betrayal hurts deeply and, whether I am right or wrong about what I am sure is happening, either way, I feel betrayed. O God, help me to deal with my emotions. And help me to begin to forgive those who are hurting me so much. Help me to overcome my sense of disappointment and anger. And, most of all, guide me that I may never betray another, even though this terrible thing is happening to me.

Give me courage to speak up if this is what is needed, or to remain silent if that is the best choice for all concerned. Guide me to understand which path is best for me to take in my situation.

I pray with all my heart in the name of Jesus who was betrayed and who chose, as a response, to forgive and love the world.
AMEN

SECTION TWO
Behaviors

CHAPTER ELEVEN.
Called to be friendly but not allowed a friend!

THE ISSUE

One of the most delicate issues about being a pastor is the matter of friendship. A pastor is required to be friendly to everyone and treat each person in the church equally. In general, pastors should not give special attention to individuals or get into personal relationships with particular people in the churches they serve. At our ordination, we vow to treat all people in the church equally.

Pastors have learned this is not as easy as it sounds. At the onset, it is common for us to arrive in a new town or city where we know no one. It's easy to start feeling lonely when we have no individual friends or old friends in the area. It is not easy to make friends with people outside the church because we are so busy with the church people that we don't have time for many outside activities. Also, friendship building takes time. But if we choose someone from the church, we're putting ourselves in line for being accused of partiality and possibly, in time, also of breaking confidences.

Even if we do not go actively seeking a special friend from the church membership, it can happen. An individual or even a couple or family may choose us for special friendship. Most church members are not spending time thinking about pastoral ethics! And most will enter friendship with us innocently. Still, there are times when a person or persons have ulterior motives. They may want to make friends with us to get some particular thing done in the church. They may be seeking a position on a board or committee. Other times, that person is lonely and wants to be a special friend of the pastor so the pastor can fill their needs. Even if all concerned have only good motives, it is still possible that other church members will be jealous of the close relationship. It is best that we seek our personal individual friends from outside the congregations we serve.

SCENARIO

Reverend Harold and his spouse Lorraine had moved to town six months ago. This town was small. It was also twelve miles from a mall, a hundred miles from a city, and five hundred miles from the church he'd last served. When they arrived, they didn't know a living soul. Most of the church members were quite friendly, but it was only the Smith family that really made a fuss over them. Mrs. Smith invited his Lorraine over to the house many times. She'd also baked pies, cookies, and her special tarts and brought them over. Mr. Smith had taken Harold fishing and to local area football games, and was just becoming a real buddy. They'd also done things as families together, but always with the Smiths treating! The Smiths had taken them to the circus and on a shopping trip into the city, and had them many times to their home for dinner.

Harold and Lorraine had been swept up in this friendship, and who could blame them? It was not until almost a year passed that they realized the Smiths may have had reasons other than friendship for their intense interest in them. It seems Mr. Smith wanted badly to be church president. Over the past five years, before Reverend Harold came to the church, Smith had tried over and over again to become president. Every time, the congregation blocked him from taking the position. For whatever reasons, they clearly did not want him to be president. The church was run by a democratic process. When Harold arrived in town, Smith had seen this as his chance. A friendship with the pastor would be just the ticket!

When the time came for the president to be chosen for the upcoming year, Smith had hoped that Reverend Harold would intercede on his behalf. Harold, not even thinking of such a thing, simply let the democratic process take its course. Smith was again not chosen. The reverend and his family were deeply hurt when, after the election, the Smiths seemed to lose interest in them. It was not long before the Smith family left the church and joined another one in the nearby town. In time, Reverend Harold was told the story of the Smiths and their quest for power. Even then it was hard for him to understand how something that felt so much like friendship could have been anything else. In time, he and his family did find friendships outside the church. And, of course, they were also able to be friendly with everyone in the church he served.

THEOLOGICAL REFLECTION

> Your trusted friends have seduced you and overcome you. (Jer 38:22b)

The prophet Jeremiah here is pointing out to King Zedekiah that he's been tricked by the people he had trusted the most. Even the most powerful people, it appears, can be hoodwinked now and again, and especially by those close to them. We pastors don't want to be untrusting, because most of the people we meet and communicate with are trustworthy. Still, when something looks too good to be true, even a friendship, maybe that's because it's not true!

As pastors we're called to be friends with all the people in our congregation, but we are discouraged from engaging in individual, personal, special friendships with any one person or family in the church. This is not always possible, but at the least we are called to try. This is not because these people are deliberately trying to get close to us for political reasons or special favors, but mainly because it's important that all be treated equally.

PRAYER

God, all that I really need is one friend. But it's not easy to find people outside the church who want to come into my life. I'm so busy with my work. Besides, in a new place, it seems that most people already have had all their friends for years, and there's no room in their lives for me. I like a lot of people at the church, and some have indicated that they'd really be happy to be my personal friend. Still, I know I need to be careful because I want to be fair to the others.

Sometimes, God, all these rules seem ridiculous. I mean, who'd really care if I simply made one personal friend from the church? Everyone is entitled to a friend. Yes, yes, I know. It's a matter of professional protocol. And yes, I also know that there's someone out there to be a friend to me—someone outside the church. Please give me patience, especially in these lonely and in between times. Help me to know that I have you for my "Forever Friend" and that, in truth, I am never alone.

Guide me also, dear God, to learn to appreciate more and more the relationships that my church members share. When two members are friends or make friends with each other for the first time, let me celebrate that and not be jealous. When I see people who are long-time friends in the church, families that share times together, let me sincerely rejoice in their happiness and realize that they see God and experience Christ through those relationships.

I pray in the name of the one who is forever both our savior and our friend, Jesus the Christ.
AMEN

CHAPTER TWELVE.
Called to love them, but I don't love that one!

THE ISSUE

We who are pastors all know perfectly well that we are supposed to love everyone in the church equally. But there is nearly always at least one that's harder to love—the one person who seems to want our blood! Well, of course that is an exaggeration, but we still feel badly about it—or maybe we feel guilty. How can we even begin to love that person who seems out to get us, or even destroy us?

We often hear the old cliché "We can love them, but nobody said we have to like them." This seems to be a manipulation, a trick. We're called to love everybody, but if, in fact, we don't like them, this would be hurtful to the person to whom we are offering this minimal kind of love. Surely God likes us too even though God may not always approve of our behavior. To love without liking seems hardly Christ-like.

Still, we must treat people fairly and kindly. We need to find ways to be good educators without being high handed. It's our job to work hard to care for, to like, and also to love our people.

SCENARIO

The day Pastor Pamela came to the church was the day it began, that non-relationship with Florence. Pamela gave her first sermon. Everyone seemed anxious to greet her on their way out of the church. Everyone shook her hand and smiled and welcomed her; everyone, that is, except Florence. Pamela's first memory of Florence was of a woman turning her head the other way and rushing past her, as if trying not to be seen. The next time they met, Florence again seemed cold and stern. Things only got worse from that point. Florence was chair of the deacons committee and seemed to disagree with Pamela on every topic that came up. Clearly, and apparently for no reason, Florence was not fond of her new pastor.

Pastor Pamela's honest reaction would have been to return this behavior with coolness on her own part. But she was supposed to be a role model. She was expected to love all her church members equally. Pamela had always wanted to be a good pastor, and she knew the rules.

One day, Florence had been particularly rude to her. Pamela tried to put aside her own hurt feelings. She pondered on the matter, and she prayed about it. Not that she hadn't done that before! But this time, some new thoughts came to mind. Maybe she looked like someone in Florence's life who had hurt her, maybe even a family member! Maybe it was because Pamela was a woman pastor, and Florence just couldn't bear the idea. Could Florence be jealous of her because she herself had no real career? Or might Florence just be one of those people they call clergy haters? Having taken the time to think about these things more clearly than she had before, Pamela realized she did not and likely could not ever really know why this woman had taken a dislike to her. She started to accept that fact. She would simply have to keep on being good to Florence while Florence kept on being bad to her.

THEOLOGICAL REFLECTION

> "I give you a new commandment, that you love one another. Just as I have loved you, you also should love one another." (John 13:34)

To love is so easy when others love us back. When their responses to us are cold and unfeeling, then we seem naturally inclined to dislike them in return. But pastors are called, above all things, to love and to demonstrate that love to all equally. With some people, loving them takes all we've got. And we don't always succeed. Still, we try to be Christlike, as best we can. Sometimes it helps us to try to remember that people may be suffering in ways we do not know, nor can we imagine. Their pain may be the reason for their negative behavior, and we have become the brunt of it through no fault of our own. Pastors are often targeted because people are angry with God but think it inappropriate or even dangerous to express their anger toward such a powerful opponent. We, of course, are not God, and are in no position to be the brunt of people's anger toward God. Still, there is little we can do. For starters, they most often do not realize who they are angry with, and certainly wouldn't believe us if we suggested it, so we can't discuss that with them. But, having an idea that the anger is not over anything we've done can greatly help us to handle it. This love thing can be complex, and we are the ones expected to understand it if anybody does. God help us in this. It is the work we do.

PRAYER

God, you know the secrets of my heart. You understand how much I want to be the best pastor I can be. But you also know how angry and upset I get with that one particular person. How can I deal with this person in a way that is equal to the others, when that one seems determined to destroy the work I do here. Help me to understand that this person is not hurting me deliberately. Something deep inside has caused such people pain, deep searing pain.

It is very likely, God, that I will never know what is bothering those people. They may not even have words themselves to tell what is hurting them.

Teach me to forgive those who hurt and seem to hate me. Teach me to realize that they too need to be understood. Help me to find ways to love and help them.

I ask this in the name of Jesus Christ who loved all of us and who died for all of us; everyone, even his enemies!

AMEN

CHAPTER THIRTEEN.
Called to confidentiality, but only on my part!

THE ISSUE

We all know the importance of confidentiality for pastors. Most or all of us have made a vow of confidentiality as part of our ordination commitment. One very real problem is that confidentiality seldom goes both ways. Individuals, church boards or committees, or other groups can call us to complete confidence, and that is normal. But in many cases they do not feel that same sense of responsibility in regard to that confidence, and that can cause huge problems for you as the pastor. For example, there is the issue of whether they will share the confidence with a spouse. Then, of course, the spouse or family member who has heard this secret is under no obligation to keep it quiet. Everyone knows that there are "leaks." When they or their family members tell the thing, they tend to forgive and forget. But if they suspect it's the pastor who spoke out, bigger trouble ensues. The pastor may be innocent or guilty but, once accused, takes the blame.

SCENARIO

"Now, I'm going to tell you this, but we must be sure it doesn't go any further," whispered Margie to Pastor Jane. "Oh, no problem, of course" was Jane's reply. "After all, I am the pastor and I am always sworn to confidentiality." All this was well and good, but the issue got further and further entangled. Before Pastor Jane knew it, she had become the victim of this secret. She was told something about another person that really needed to be out in the open. She, of course, did not disclose it to a soul. But, through others, it came out anyway. The next thing she heard, they were talking about her, suggesting not so subtly that the secret had indeed been exposed by her, that she had known all along. Some said she must have been the one who told others, and what kind of pastor might she be if she couldn't even keep confidences shared with her? Others were saying the opposite, but also against her; suggesting that she had kept a secret that she should not have kept, and which needed to be out for the wellbeing of the church. She was in a classic no-win situation. It took Pastor Jane some time to figure out what had happened to her and just how it had come about. What she'd learned is that too many church members will use the confidentiality promise on the part of the pastor to their own ends. She was trapped, metaphorically, between a rock and a hard place. If she'd refused to say that she'd keep the confidence, what kind of a pastor would she be? If she revealed it, that would be even worse. She learned the hard way that pastors must choose the path that will help them avoid these kinds of issues. Many times, when there are confidences to be kept, it is equally important for the church member(s) to keep them as well.

THEOLOGICAL REFLECTION

> But whenever you pray, go into your room and shut the door and pray to your Father who is in secret, and your Father who sees in secret will reward you. (Matt 6:6)

This passage is, of course, about prayer, and we are called to do our praying in private as opposed to making an outward show of our religious piety. But it also says something about the work we do as pastors. The quiet and the confidential work is more important, in many instances, than the outward show. A lot of what we do happens in secret. While in other businesses, people are praised and lifted up for their overt good work, so much of what we do in our labor as pastors is in secret. We see people, and we listen to their troubles and confessions. We pray with them, and later we pray for them. None of this is witnessed by others.

Confidentiality is one of the most important aspects of the ordained ministry. When people have no place to go to share their confessions or their troubles, they will come to you, the pastor, knowing and trusting that their secrets will stay with you. But it is important to know that confidences can be used by church members in various ways to get the pastor in trouble. The reason for any confidence needs to be clear, and the confidentiality decision must be made by both parties and for reasons that will not hurt others.

PRAYER

God, you hold so many of my confidences. You are the one I know I can come to with all the secrets of my heart. Here is my plea today. Help me to discern when it is best to promise confidentiality and when that may not be right or appropriate.

Help me to use my own good judgment, my own best life experiences, and my own goodwill in making these kinds of decisions.

I know and trust that you love us beyond all measure and that you forgive us and always give us new chances to do what is right. Grant my people the courage and the wisdom to trust you in this way as well. And, in as open a way as possible, may we work together to make a better church and a better world.

May Jesus' good judgment influence me and the decisions I make. I pray in the name of Jesus who knows all my secrets and loves me just the same.

AMEN

CHAPTER FOURTEEN.
Called to lead, but everybody's my boss!

THE ISSUE

Too often, in parish ministry, the pastor is treated as an employee instead of a preacher, teacher, and leader. If you are in this situation, you very likely did not cause it. The situation may often reflect an inappropriate relationship in this regard between this congregation and their previous pastor or an earlier pastor. For example, the earlier pastor may have been weak in the leadership department and the people may have had to take over certain aspects of the church's work. On the other hand, it could simply be that these church members came out of a congregational tradition in which the pastor was expected to keep his or her place, that being in the pulpit, and let the people do the leg work. Either way, for you as the current pastor who must deal with this problem, it is very real!

One way such an issue can be dealt with is from the pulpit. Without being specific, your sermons over a period of time might reflect such things as the importance of "calling" and what it actually means to be set apart for ordained ministry. It is possible that the people really think it's their responsibility to be your employers. After all, their work lives reflect the rules of the marketplace, which are quite different from the way things are done in a loving worshiping community.

SCENARIO

Mary dropped by the church office on Monday morning to remind Pastor Nan that there would be a meeting that night to discuss the recent financial issues. She even prepped her on some suggestions about what Nan should do to alleviate the problem. Pastor Nan didn't really mind, although she certainly didn't need any reminders about that meeting. Still, she wondered exactly what made Mary think it was any of her business, as Mary was not on any committee. On Wednesday, Nan got no fewer than three phone calls from church members telling her to visit a church member who was in the hospital. That was nice, but Nan did not need the prompt. She had all the information she needed before any of them called and had already been to the hospital first thing that morning. In addition to this, she had church members advising her on any number of matters for which she really didn't need help, not to mention their continuously sending her on errands all over town on behalf of the church, and instructing her on exactly how the church should be run. She was especially annoyed at a man named Thomas who gave the impression he thought he should really be the pastor and not Nan. Well, maybe Thomas didn't want to be the pastor himself, but he certainly did have the idea that somehow, he was Pastor Nan's boss! She tried to keep cool, but she couldn't help but think how strange it was. She had always imagined her role as pastor would get her some respect and had greatly looked forward to serving a church. Her experience was turning out to be much the opposite. Far too many church members really did seem to think they were her boss.

THEOLOGICAL REFLECTION

> Then Moses ordered Israel to set out from the Red Sea, and they went into the wilderness of Shur. They went for three days in the wilderness and found no water. When they came to Marah, they could not drink the water of Marah because it was bitter. That is why it was called

Marah. And the people complained against Moses, saying, "What shall we drink?" (Exod 15:22–24)

In this text, the people are complaining. They all think they know better than Moses. They were perfectly willing to follow him out of Egypt and into the desert, but now, as soon as they are freed, they have started complaining.

One of the biggest problems of leadership is that too many people who have too little information think they know better than the leader. As pastors, we put up with a lot of this kind of behavior without complaining. This does not mean we have to take the advice or give in to every whim our people may have. In the case of Moses, even though the people were out of order in complaining, they also happened to be right. The water was indeed bitter, and action was needed. Moses must have also reminded himself that the people had given up everything to follow him. When people are telling us pastors about how to do our job, it can be very frustrating. Still, many of them have been in the church longer than we have. Some have experience in the world that can assist us in our ministry. Others may just be feeling powerless and need a sense of power or influence over someone! We need to try to discern their reasons and decide how best to respond, without getting angry and frustrated with them. It is never easy, but it seems to be part of the important "people work" that pastors are called to do.

PRAYER

Great God, the truth is that it never occurred to me once when I was in seminary that I could end up working for two hundred bosses at the same time. Well, maybe that's an exaggeration, but it's the way it feels right now. Didn't they call me to be their leader? At the very least, they did agree at my installation service that I was to be their "pastor and teacher." A pastor can preach the gospel and even admonish. A teacher guides the people to learn more. But these days too often I feel like I'm everybody's servant and, worse yet, everybody's employee! Yes, I know they're paying my salary, but that was never intended to be the focus, only a way for me to survive while I lead and share with them out of love, with you as my boss!

Give me strength and grace to lead this congregation into a better relationship with me in this regard. Help me to understand their motivations when they try to be my boss. Remind me when I want to blame them that it possibly might not be their fault. Help me to love them as I gently move them to a new "place"; one in which they truly respect their pastor, and trust what I am doing.

And, God, no doubt there are also times that these church members are right in trying to guide me. Give me the discernment to know when this is the case, and to heed their advice or follow their directions.

I ask all this in the name of Jesus who always spoke with authority but who also always kept in close connection with his one and only boss!

AMEN

CHAPTER FIFTEEN.
Called to mission but required to "keep the lights on"

THE ISSUE

In most churches, the pastor's written or unwritten "job description" does include having to stay carefully within the budget while also taking responsibility to some extent for the continued fiscal survival and "success" of the organization. Certainly, in the case of just about any church, if things go downhill financially, it's the pastor who'll be the first to be blamed.

It's not that there is anything particularly wrong with this, but in many cases it can be time consuming and worrisome, and it can take away from the pursuit of our true vocation. You won't be studying Scripture when you are too distracted continually having to pour over church budget sheets.

SCENARIO

The congregation, or at least the trustees and council members of Acre Road Church, seemed totally distracted by matters of money. The budget was not being met! This was the second year in a row! As the financial concerns of the leadership mounted, it seemed that the entire congregation was looking for somebody to blame.

The pastor was a good one, faithful to his calling and to his denomination. Nevertheless, it was that same pastor who began to be blamed. This was strange as there was little doubt that the church members could quite easily have opened their pockets and given more generously without undue suffering. Instead, they chose to find a scapegoat—the pastor. They said he was not showing enough interest in finances. His sermons were not drawing in new members. A certain couple with substantial resources had recently left the church. It was so easy to blame the pastor.

In the end, that pastor left the church for another calling. The congregation managed to actually save quite a few dollars on their budget during the period when they did not have to sustain a full-time pastor with housing, medical, and pension requirements. By the time two years had passed, they chose a new pastor who was willing to work for a lower wage, and everything seemed to be resolved. In truth, it was not resolved, because what had really been needed was an increase in giving from the congregation. If each family or individual had increased their pledge by only a few dollars, they would not have had to lose their perfectly good pastor or spend two years in limbo searching for a new one. The new pastor was no more a financial leader than the one they'd had. In a few years, they were back with the same issue, and they would continue with this cycle until they were willing to admit to themselves that financial responsibility was something that had to be shared between congregants and the pastor.

THEOLOGICAL REFLECTION

> When he [Elijah] came to the gate of the town, a widow was there gathering sticks; he called to her and said, "Bring me a little water in a vessel, so that I may drink." As she was going to bring it, he called to her and said, "Bring me a morsel of bread in your hand." But she said, "As the Lord your God lives, I have nothing baked, only a handful of meal in a jar, and a little oil in a jug; I am now gathering a couple of sticks so that I may go home

and prepare it for myself and my son, that we may eat it and die." Elijah said to her, "Do not be afraid; go out and do as you have said, but first make me a little cake of it and bring it to me, and afterward make something for yourself and your son. For thus says the Lord the God of Israel: the jar of meal will not be emptied, and the jug of oil will not fail until the day that the Lord sends rain upon the earth." She went and did as Elijah said, so that she as well as he and her household ate for many days. (1 Kgs 17:10b–15)

The point of this story is abundance. As the story begins, the woman has no hope. After Elijah's visit, her needs are met. The prophet Elijah shows up and asks the woman, who has nothing, to feed him. What can this mean? Is the prophet being selfish? No. He is using this request to teach that God will provide, that God always meets needs. And, as we might expect, God does exactly that.

"And do not keep seeking what you are to eat and what you are to drink, and do not keep worrying. For it is the nations of the world that seek all these things, and your Father knows that you need them. Instead, seek his kingdom, and these things will be given to you as well" (Luke 12:29–30).

Here, in the New Testament, Jesus reminds us that we should not worry so much about the material things that we forget about what is truly important: the kingdom of God. When we have our priorities right, the rest will surely follow.

PRAYER

God, after all the amazing things I learned in seminary, I end up with them expecting me to be a high financier! We didn't study a thing about money in seminary, except for the words of Jesus that we "give therefore to Caesar the things that are Caesar's and to God the things that are God's" (Matt 22:21b). Help me to guide my people to understand what my real work is among them in this place; and that is to make you known, to make your love a reality for them, and to help them realize that you always provide.

Guide me to be the best pastor in every way—yes, even including financial matters.

I ask this in the name of Jesus who taught us to "seek first the kingdom of God and his righteousness, and all these things will be given to you as well" (Matt 6:33). Help us all to remember the things that really count.

AMEN

CHAPTER SIXTEEN.
Called to a church but running a "country club"

THE ISSUE

Sit down sometime and make a two-sided list: pros and cons. Is your church starting to seem more like a country club? If the answer is no, consider yourself a lucky and blessed pastor. If the answer is yes, then you are not alone. Here are a few of the questions that will lead you to the answer.

Are my people coming to church when they feel like it instead of when they need to, or do most of them attend on a regular basis?

Are we more concerned about building repairs and renovations to our facility than we are about the very important human issues?

Is it possible there are people in our area who do not come to our church because they think they can't afford it?

Do our programs seem to be for the current members rather than newcomers who might find their way to our doors?

At budget time, what are the priorities? Do they reflect helping those in need in our own area, missions for other countries, finding new members, guiding children? Or are they focused more on comfort and perks for current members?

SCENARIO

It was a long time before Reverend Jack had become willing to admit to himself that his church had more or less turned into a country club. Of course, he'd known when he came that the church was located in an affluent area. And, yes, he had noticed that they were lacking throughout their history in any "hands on" kind of ministry to the poor or the downtrodden. But now, in Jack's opinion, things were starting to go too far. The council had actually voted against his recommendation to prepare lunches for the homeless shelter on Saturday mornings. They had voted against the opportunity offered to have physically challenged children meet there on Sunday afternoons. The council had agreed they would ask the A.A. group to find a new place to meet. It's not that the congregation was doing anything particularly wrong. But they seemed not to be growing in the faith, in the pastor's opinion, at least regarding "faith in action." The church had plenty of activities, but they all seemed to be for the enjoyment of its members. New membership was not encouraged. They were happy with each other and had suggested more than once that it would be good if Pastor Jack could go out into the community and try to find "people who are like us." Pastor Jack knew it was time for a change, although the people had not yet come to that realization.

The change did happen. After a further year of trying to suggest a variety of ministry projects for the congregation, Pastor Jack went out himself seeking a new project—another church to serve, one that really cared! He might have tried to change the congregation, but he chose to give himself a chance with a more mission-minded church and also give this congregation another chance. With a different leader, they might come out of their sleep and move in new directions.

THEOLOGICAL REFLECTION

> For I was hungry, and you gave me no food, I was thirsty, and you gave me nothing to drink, I was a stranger, and you did not welcome me, naked and you did not give

me clothing, sick and in prison and you did not visit me. Then, they also will answer "Lord, when was it that we saw you hungry or thirsty or a stranger or naked or sick or in prison and did not take care of you?" Then he will answer them, "Truly I tell you, just as you did not do it to one of the least of these, you did not do it to me." (Matt 25:42–45)

Most often we hear the text of Matthew's Gospel that comes immediately before this one—the positive side of the story, which tells us that when we do good things for the least of the brothers and sisters, we are doing them for God. We seldom think about this reverse side; that, should we do nothing, we are withholding from God, and God may be displeased with us. If we want to truly be among God's people, we will want to act in ways that serve those who need us the most. We will no longer be self-serving and unwilling to open our lives and selves and our resources to others.

PRAYER

Great God, you call us Christians to go into the world and serve. It seems too often to me that my people are interested in self-serving and in having me serve them! Help me to be a role model and a guide to them in this regard. Give me wisdom in my preaching so that, without being obvious or nagging, I can lead us together into a deeper sense of mission toward those around us, and to our whole world.

Help me to realize too, dear God, that, just because these church members do have the right to enjoy their church life together, that doesn't make them a country club! I mean, they need community, and they need each other. As their leader, don't let me forget that they are also called to meet each other's needs. Still, as they enjoy working and celebrating with each other, may they also open their hearts to visitors and new people in our church community, and to our world outside our doors.

I ask this in the name of Jesus who always welcomed the stranger and who taught us to be as children.
AMEN

CHAPTER SEVENTEEN.
Called to be a community leader but expected to stay in my office

THE ISSUE

One of the major dilemmas that nobody ever talks about in ministry is that many church members have an unreasonable expectation of their pastor, expecting you to be in two places at a given time! We're in religion, not magic! There are the people who expect and almost demand that their pastor be out in the community, serving on local committees that address any number of issues: community building, caring for the poor, dealing with trying to end racism and bigotry, school boards, and who knows what else. At the same time, there are others, or sometimes even the same people, who fully expect the pastor to be in the office, working hard, and available to meet people, answer phones, or simply be present, whether or not anyone wants or needs to see them.

How will you deal with this? Well, very likely you know best where you should be and how many "outside" groups you ought to appropriately serve for the sake your church and your best ministry. No one can know better how you should be using your work time. Once this has been determined, then you simply need to go ahead with conviction. It's a good idea for you try to keep the congregation informed about the things you're doing. If they receive regular reports from you, they too may feel connected and even want to go with you to be part of the outside committees and events you are involved in. Any time you can work together with a church member or members toward building up a better community or world, your ministry is enhanced.

SCENARIO

Marv loved most everything about being a pastor. He enjoyed his office work, the preaching, the counseling, and the time he spent eating pizza with the teens of the church. But Marv had to admit, what he loved more than anything else related to his ministerial calling was the work he did outside the church building, the work that contributed to making a better town and a stronger community. It was not long after coming to the church that he'd been invited to the newly formed town race relations committee. He did such a good job in building up that group that within a year he found himself on the board of trustees for a local boarding school for troubled teens. In addition, he had belonged for years to the Rotary Club. All this, to some extent, was his private business but, he felt, also good for the church. The trouble was, having put all these good activities together, certain members of his church started talking! How could Pastor Marv be doing his work for the church when he was out of the office so much? Whose interests was he representing? Where were his priorities? Some had called the offices and waited an hour or more before they received a response from him.

Now, what was Marv to do? Surely, he couldn't just quit everything and sit in the church all day waiting for those particular people just in case they might want to speak to him. But could he go on with his "outside" ministries without repercussions? One thing was sure—Marv was going to lose some sleep over this one!

THEOLOGICAL REFLECTION

> And Jesus came and said to them, "All authority in heaven and on earth has been given to me. Go therefore and make disciples of all nations, baptizing them in the name of the Father and of the Son and of the Holy Spirit and teaching them everything that I have commanded you. And remember, I am with you always to the end of the age." (Matt 28:18–20)

The key to this passage in relation to this particular study is the action verb, "Go!" All of us, as Christians, are called to keep moving forward, not to withdraw from the world in meditation for the glory of God but, rather, to be God's faithful people in the world.

If we can assume that the people in our congregations are already Christians, then we and they need to do much of our work out in the world, in our communities, for good and for change in the name of the Christ whom we serve. We know as called and ordained pastors that we are not only shepherds to the people in our churches, but also role models and workers for the building of the kingdom, as it is lived out and expressed in our own neighborhoods and larger communities. Still, we pastors need to strike a balance between our inside work and our outside work. We also must find ways to educate our congregations, so that they understand what we are doing and why we are doing it. Maybe, once they understand more and know they are needed, they will also seek to join us in much of that outside work.

PRAYER

O God, you know my heart! Everything I do, I try to do for your greater glory, and in the name of the church that I am serving. Why don't they understand? Why do I get the uneasy feeling that they think I'm wasting time or serving my own personal interests when I go out to work so hard on behalf of our church and our community?

Being a Rock in a Hard Place

Make me feel more in control over this issue, O powerful Creator. Help me to remember they have a right to be kept informed about my "outside the church building" activities. And, if I have indeed taken on too much, then make me see that clearly and make the appropriate adjustments needed. I want to be the best pastor I can be for them, and I want to keep a good balance of work-related activities. Give me strength to do your work in a way that is both right and pleasing in your sight.

I pray all this in the name of Jesus, who so often went outside his area and beyond his borders to do the work of the Holy One.
AMEN

CHAPTER EIGHTEEN.
Called to model for the Joneses but expected to keep up with them

THE ISSUE

One common problem that comes up in parish ministry is that a pastor's salary does not always permit the pastor to realistically keep up with the church members' lifestyle. In principle, such a salary may fit perfectly into denominational guidelines. But there are often extenuating circumstances that make it difficult for the pastor's family to manage on the salary that is given. Here is a short list of possible reasons.

The pastor may be paying off a rather large student loan from attending seminary.

The pastor may have children in college or elderly parents who have to be cared for.

The pastor or his/her family member may have costly health related issues.

The area sometimes has particularly high real estate values.

The congregation may have a high income level or be wealthy for other reasons. Often the people in the congregation expect their pastor to live a lifestyle that is similar to their own.

It's not that the pastor is trying to "keep up with the Joneses" or even wants to do so. It's just that the congregational members don't realize they are involved in such high living. For them it's just a normal lifestyle they've, in many cases, experienced all their lives. A new pastor comes in and, especially at the outset, tends to feel he or she should at least look like he or she lives a similar lifestyle. For example, the house the family purchases might be expected to have enough space to hold occasional meetings, a church Christmas gathering, or youth group events. Generally, even if most everything does take place at the church, the pastor's home is seen as a place people are curious about and would like to visit on occasion. This also means you need decent furniture that fits in well with the house and neighborhood. Then, there is the matter of the car. We don't need a Cadillac or a Hummer! After all, everyone knows we are modeling some level of frugality. Still, what might the people at the other church down the street think if they see the pastor of our church driving a clunker? In addition, some congregations expect their pastor to attend the symphony orchestra concerts. Others might be mortified if good old Pastor Bob didn't go to the football game. Different strokes! But none of them come cheap. We pastors can accept a few "freebees," but then comes our turn to treat or at least to pay our own way. If we try to get out of it, well, we are just being tight.

SCENARIO

The Rodriguez family did need a rather large house. This had not been a problem at their last parish, as a rather large parsonage had been provided. Of course, that meant a lower salary for Pastor Miguel, but they had managed. Now they'd moved to DC, and the real estate costs had been a bit higher than they expected. It was only a few months before they realized they were going to be short of cash. A number of uncontrollable factors contributed to the problem. They had bought the large house and discovered that the roof had to be replaced. The window frames turned out to be the old type and allowed too much heat to escape with the result that their heating bill was almost double what it had been before they moved there. Maria, Miguel's wife, could no longer go to work on a subway, so they had to purchase and maintain a second car. Add to that the congregation's expectation that the family would attend all sorts of costly social events, and the result was something close to financial disaster. At first, they thought there was nothing they could do. But, after one year, they got together as a family and made a crucial decision. They put their big house on the market, found a smaller one in an adjoining lower-priced neighborhood, and simply moved! To their surprise, the congregation didn't ask a lot of questions. They also accepted that their pastor did not live exactly the way they did, but that he was still able to love and serve them in every way they needed. They were perfectly happy with their pastor and his family. They'd never really needed him to live the same lifestyle they lived but, because they had never expressed it, he had no way of knowing that.

THEOLOGICAL REFLECTION

> Then someone came to him and said, "Teacher, what good deed must I do to have eternal life?" And he said to him, "Why do you ask me about what is good? There is one who is good. If you wish to enter into life, keep the commandments." He said to him, "Which ones?" And Jesus said, "You shall not murder, You shall not commit adultery; You shall not steal. You shall not bear false witness. Honor your father and mother. Also, you shall love your neighbor as yourself." The young man said to him, "I have kept all these; what do I still lack?" Jesus said to him, "If you wish to be perfect, go, sell your possessions, and give the money to the poor, and you will have treasure in heaven; then, come, follow me." When the young man heard this word, he went away grieving, for he had many possessions. (Matt 19:16–22)

This is such a touching story. The rich young man, it appears, is just unable to give up everything and follow Jesus. He has followed all the rules for living but cannot take that last step. There is much to be learned from this passage. Accumulation of money is not what life is about. Neither is simply following all the rules.

If we truly want abundant life, we seek the kingdom of God and heavenly treasures. But it is not easy to do so.

PRAYER

God, you know me. You know my heart is pure, and I have never been one to particularly seek after wealth or material things. Still, somehow, I've become caught up in spending more than I can really afford and living a lifestyle that seems to be beyond my means. I wouldn't say I do it to impress my church members, but it seems that they have been expecting me to keep up with their lifestyle.

Help me to believe and know that the people I serve will accept me as I am. Guide me to realize that, as their religious leader, my work is not to copy them, but to model better possibilities for them.

I pray in the name of Jesus who said, "Foxes have holes, and birds of the air have nests, but the Son of Man has nowhere to lay his head" (Matt 8:20), and yet he was the greatest of all role models.

AMEN

CHAPTER NINETEEN.
Called by a search committee with an agenda other than that of the congregation

THE ISSUE

They told you who they were and what their goals were, and they described to you the dreams of this congregation. That pastoral search committee also chose exactly the right person for the job they described, and that person was you! You took up the mandate and set to work to help fulfill their dreams. So, why then is there a problem now? Strangely enough, the answer is simple. There are two reasons. First, search committees are often chosen from people who are not on other committees, resulting in the fact that these people do not always know the church members' real agendas. Secondly, even if this committee conducted a full survey of every member of the congregation, they still may not come up with truly honest answers. It's not that people are intentionally telling lies. But church members tend too often to give the answer they feel they "should" give, instead of their true feelings. The result is that you may very well be striving hard to reach goals that the congregation cares little about or, even worse, goals that in truth they do not want to happen!

SCENARIO

The one thing the Little Church on the Hill thought it wanted most of all was children! Most of the congregation consisted of older people whose children had long been married and gone. Their own grandchildren nearly all lived in other areas or were not brought to church by their parents. The neighborhood was inhabited mostly by seniors. When Pastor Jim came to this church, he was told he'd been chosen because he loved working with children and youth. He'd been so happy to accept because he loved working with children! The problem was that, once he got started there, he came rather quickly to realize that few people in the congregation had any interest in children at all. As a matter of fact, every time he got new young families to come to the church, many members seemed quite agitated by the presence of the children. He even got complaints. A child was being too noisy in worship. Sunday school expenses were going up, and the trustees were complaining that it was the children's fault that the church was over budget. Nobody wanted to teach the kids because Sunday school was at the same time as the one Sunday service. When he suggested a change in the time schedule, that was met with a strong and clear negative response.

In short, the special work that Pastor Jim had been assigned to accomplish by the pastoral search committee turned out to be work that was of little or no concern to the actual congregation! How did this happen? Actually, it is not that surprising. Search committee members who, as I mentioned earlier, may not have served on other committees are often not the best judges of the congregation's real wishes and needs. On the other hand, it may be surprising to know that, when congregations are asked to fill out forms about their desires, they do not always express them honestly, for fear of sounding selfish or inconsiderate.

THEOLOGICAL REFLECTION

> And Amaziah said to Amos, "O seer, go, flee away to the land of Judah, earn your bread there, and prophesy there; but never again prophesy at Bethel, for it is the king's sanctuary, and it is a temple of the kingdom." Then Amos answered Amaziah, "I am no prophet, nor a prophet's son; but I am a herdsman and a dresser of sycamore trees, and the Lord took me from following the flock, and the Lord said to me, 'Go, prophesy to my people Israel.'" (Amos 7:12–15)

In this passage, Amaziah has one idea of what Amos should be doing. Amos has another. And, God has yet another. Amos does not see himself as a prophet, and, if he stays at his regular work, he will continue as some kind of shepherd and vineyard keeper. Amaziah, on the other hand, sees Amos as a prophet but doesn't want him to be plying his trade in this area! God, however, has the upper hand, and has decided that this is exactly where Amos needs to be as a prophet: not being one of those so-called prophets paid by kings to tell them what they want to hear, but a prophet called by God to tell them what Almighty God wants them to hear.

As pastors, we can easily get confused, trying to discern between the expectations of people in our churches and the requirements of God. We've been trained to study Scripture and listen for the "sound of sheer silence" (1 Kgs 19:12b). We see ourselves as called by God to the work we do. Yet we have so many voices, and sometimes conflicting voices, advising us as to what is important and what is less so. Then there is the matter of whether we choose to do what the people say they want, what they probably really want, what we think is best for them, or maybe something quite different.

PRAYER

God, you know that I know what they said they wanted for this church. And I know that you know that I have done exactly that, to the best of my ability. Now, I feel confused because it feels too often that I am fighting uphill to get anything done in this regard.

Help me to understand these people I serve. If this direction that I've been taking is right for the church, give me courage to stay the course. If it needs to change, then help me to know how and when to make such changes.

It is difficult for us pastors to know when to continue with the way we are doing things, and when to change or adjust our plans. Help me to keep the lines of communication open between me and my church members. Give me wisdom to discern their real needs so I can serve them better.

I ask this in the name of Jesus who always knew what people needed before they asked and who knows best the needs of both this congregation and its pastor, even before we ask.

AMEN

CHAPTER TWENTY.
Called to those who say they support me but disappear when the chips are down

THE ISSUE

It is an unfortunate fact that many people are not willing to stand up for what they say they believe in, especially when the time comes to support or protect another person at their own expense. When this happens in the church setting, and it's the pastor or the pastor's will that they are not willing to support, then this can be very hurtful to the pastor.

There are reasons why people may choose not to support the pastor, reasons the pastor seldom thinks of. For example, one major reason is that they realize that, in some ways, the pastor is the one person in the church who is somehow "just passing through," while the people with whom they are in relationship in the congregation are liable to be in that place over the very long haul. Should any individual take sides with the pastor against the others, even if the pastor is right, the price to pay can be high. This is the stuff that church splits are made of, and they can be very serious. The relationships among the people in any congregation are important to the members. Deep friendships are often forged within congregations, and many church members have long mutual histories.

For this reason, there are cases in which the pastor—as right as he or she may be in any disagreement—is likely to take the fall!

Yes, you may be disappointed and extremely surprised when people seem to choose any side but yours in a disagreement. But it is often best to bite the bullet and let the matter go. Feeling angry with them can only hurt both them and you. Yes, you may end up being there for thirty years, but in today's ministerial climate, it is more likely your ministry there will be six to ten years, tops.

SCENARIO

Pastor Ken was in some trouble, but he felt everything would probably come out alright in the end. If he had learned one thing back in his seminary days, it was how important it is not to let any church split over you, the pastor. Still, without his having been able to control it, people had been taking sides for and against an important issue. The issue in this case was a decision to purchase new pews. Well, they were not exactly pews, but rather they were linking chairs. Bringing these chairs into the sanctuary would certainly change the mood of the place. Some believed this would be a modernization and attract new members. Those who took the opposite side believed that this change would destroy the entire sense of holiness in the sanctuary. Some had already threatened to leave if it ever happened. Pastor Ken wished he'd never brought up the subject in the first place! He'd been the one who wanted the new chairs. Ken had been thinking that new chairs could be shifted into different configurations to meet various needs. Also, he felt the more contemporary look in the sanctuary would be a welcome change and make people feel more at home and also closer to each other.

The possibility of a split congregation over the relatively unimportant issue of seating, however, was not what ended up surprising Pastor Ken the most. No! It was what happened when the vote came in. The council had decided to take it to the congregation for an open vote of hands, to take place at a short meeting following the worship service. Ken had decided to go along with the decision of the people, but he never guessed it would go this way. He'd spent many hours over the past month explaining why he believed the new chairs would be a good decision for the church. And many of the congregation had agreed with him, both privately and even in front of others. His best advocate, Simon, had heartily agreed. Simon had assured the pastor of his support for the project and even suggested he would make a sizable donation. In addition, his good friends Marv and John had both joked with him about how many configurations the chairs might take for various occasions! Pastor Ken did not know if his idea for the chairs would win the vote, but he was convinced there would be, at the least, a very close vote!

To his very great surprise, the vote came in, and it was unanimous. The hands were being raised, one after another. "All in favor of keeping the old pews and NOT buying chairs, raise your hand." The people looked around at one another and, one after another, began raising their hands. Before two minutes had passed, every hand in the church was raised. It was declared unanimous! The pews would stay. Ken could not believe his eyes. This was simply impossible. As prepared as he had been to lose, he had never prepared for this decision.

The blow to Pastor Ken's ego did not do him any harm. But his trust level that his people meant what they said was shaken. Some time later, he came to see that there might have been any number of reasons why the people did not go along with his idea when it came down to the vote. Those who had planned to vote in favor of the new chairs may have become nervous when they saw so many hands going up to keep the pews and must have decided they'd better go along with the winning team. Then, of course, there is also the fact that tradition is important to many churchgoers. In this case, it may have been their memories of sitting in church pews, however uncomfortable or impractical, that brought them to change their minds and vote to keep old pews and maintain their old ways. Ken came to realize in time that their vote against the chairs was not a vote against him.

Being a Rock in a Hard Place

THEOLOGICAL REFLECTION

> Then he came to the disciples and found them sleeping, and he said to Peter, "So, could you not stay awake with me one hour? Stay awake and pray that you may not come into the time of trial; the spirit indeed is willing, but the flesh is weak." ... Again, he came and found them sleeping, for their eyes were heavy. (Matt 26:40–43)

The disciples did not stand with Jesus when the chips were down. Peter denied him three times almost immediately after vowing his undying loyalty. In the above passage, they fall asleep when Jesus most needs their support in prayer and presence. He points it out to them but does not later blame or hold a grudge. The disciples are prone to the foibles of the human condition and therefore choose to follow their selfish interests and relieve their fatigue with a nap, giving that nap precedence over their intense loyalty to Jesus.

We pastors are often privy to a close look at the imperfection of human behavior. We can take a lesson from Jesus here. He does not condone the nonsupport of his closest followers, and he is not pleased, but neither does he blame them.

PRAYER

O Holy One, help me to stop thinking that people are against me just because they don't always agree with me. Help me also to understand my people when they do not do what they say they were going to do or vote the way they said they were going to vote in our church matters.

It is our privilege as free humans to change our minds, even at the last minute. I afford myself that privilege; may I do so equally for others.

God, you know that I have always tried to discern what is best for our church. I have been so sure that what I wanted was best for all. So many of the people seemed to agree and then, to my great surprise and disappointment, they turn away. I feel deserted.

CALLED TO THOSE WHO SAY THEY SUPPORT ME

I feel angry too. I have even wanted to call them "traitors" and "turncoats," even "Judases." Forgive me. Help me to understand that they have many reasons for not choosing my ways or wanting to agree with my judgments. Give me the sense to know that, in many cases, they have been here longer than I, and that, perhaps, they will also be here long after I have gone my way! Over this issue, God, these people and I disagree, but there are many things we do agree on.

God, we are all your people together! Together, we constitute your holy Church. We are your servants. Open your will to us together, so that we may proceed with shared good judgment.

Help me to know that, when I am supported by others or even when they let me down, I always have a friend in Jesus, in whose name I offer this prayer.

AMEN

CHAPTER TWENTY-ONE.
Called to be a "nice young family," but my family can't bear it!

THE ISSUE

It may be true that the average congregation will want to choose a pastor who is a "nice young man with a wife who preferably plays the piano, and two or three lovely and well-behaved children." Today, the pastor they get will seldom fit such a profile. More and more, pastoral search committees are finding the best person fitted to serve their congregation is a second-career person, a single or married woman, someone of another race from themselves, or a person with physical challenges. Still, even the classic pastor with a spouse and young family may find the ministry incredibly challenging. For one thing, there are usually too many different expectations from different church members. So, what do you do and how do you cope when it is not you but your beloved family who can't bear life in the fishbowl—the life of parish ministry—one they did not choose for themselves?

SCENARIO

John's spouse Maria said she understood when he left his rather successful IT job to go to the seminary. She had been willing to

Called to Be a "Nice Young Family,"

accompany him to the city and to work part time while also caring for their two young children while he was doing his studies. That brought much joy for them as a family. He'd enjoyed his classes and his studies, and they had a rather nice social life with the other young married couples like themselves also struggling through the years of seminary education.

But things had changed for the worse once John was ordained and took a church. Maria and their son and daughter had been warmly welcomed when they first arrived, but things were turning. The congregation, it appeared, had expected Maria to work for them without benefit of any remuneration. She didn't really mind, but surely her time was worth something! In addition, much to her surprise, she'd heard that some of the people seemed to resent her being on the Christian education committee. She'd even overheard one woman on that committee complaining to another that Maria was just there to support her husband's off-the-wall ideas, and that no pastor's spouse should get involved in the church's affairs. Maria loved these people just as her husband did. Maria had labored in the church kitchen when her own dishes remained unwashed in the kitchen sink at home. But now she had just had enough! The problem was, as the pastor's wife, she really couldn't voice her opinions. She had to be "nice" just as her husband was nice. This was the behavior expected of the pastor's spouse.

The same went for the children. Their daughter, Linda, was a good girl, but she was expected to be some kind of perfect role model for all teenage girls in the congregation. That was a high expectation, and Linda occasionally fell short. The same was true for Gavin, the son. People at church seemed to be monitoring who his friends were at school, not to mention where he went in the evenings. The feeling seemed to be that, if the kids didn't meet everyone's expectations, then Pastor John and spouse Maria, the parents, were to blame.

The pressure was not something that could be openly observed or talked about. It was subtle and began to wear on them as a family. They couldn't find a real solution to the problem because it had so many faces! Finally, they decided to get together as a family and have what they called their "Secret Sunday Evening Ragging Sessions." Around 9 p.m. every Sunday, they committed to sit down as a family and have an absolutely confidential secret meeting in which each one had the opportunity to tell his or her stories of the week and express their feelings without fear of repercussions. Little changed over the coming years that could be outwardly seen. But, the result of these family meetings was that they could go back into the fray every Monday with a feeling of solidarity. While they indeed did complain quite a lot about the people of the church, they also reminded themselves at every one of those meetings, at the start and at the finish, that they had been called by God to love and serve them. This congregation may not have known it, but it was truly blessed. (Instead of just one pastor, they ended up with a whole family who cared for them and felt love for them.)

THEOLOGICAL REFLECTION

> The Lord bless you from Zion. May you see the prosperity of Jerusalem all the days of your life. May you see your children's children. Peace be upon Israel. (Ps 128:5–6)

To see our children happy and successful is the dream of every parent, pastors of course included. We are all aware that our children are not perfect, only human. Growing up is not easy, and it's normal and it's expected that the young ones will go through some stages of growth that may be difficult or embarrassing. Church members do not always think of this, as their own children may have been long past those difficult ages. Congregations are known to often be over-demanding with their expectations for the pastor's children, thinking they ought to be junior role models for the rest. And sometimes they are! Still, we can be happy to know simply that our children, although far from perfect, still are perfectly okay.

PRAYER

God of all that is, hear my prayer. I am so frustrated and so tired. I ask for your help, not for myself but for my family. It was I and not they who chose this life of ministry and service. They are serving you too, of course, but they are in this often-difficult life because of me. Help me to serve my precious family as well as my church members. Help me never to forget how important my family is to me and to the work that I do in your service. Give my precious family strength and courage. If I find it necessary to talk with my church members about how they are treating my family, give me the courage and grace to do it in a way that is pleasing to you.

As Jesus said we are all family, help us to love and care for each other, in his name.

AMEN

CHAPTER TWENTY-TWO.
Called to admonish, preach, and teach but expected to appease, please, and entertain

THE ISSUE

When we were in seminary it was made very clear to us that our call was two-fold and consisted of preaching and teaching! When we were ordained, this is exactly what we promised to do. We looked forward to it, understanding that we were to always be educators. This meant we were to remember we were educators not only in the pulpit but also in the classroom or workshop, in committee meetings, and even in conversation with church members. Even though this did not mean we were to act as some kind of authority figures, there would often be opportunities to guide and lead as their pastor.

Yet, in far too many cases, a congregation is not happy unless we are telling them what they want and expect to hear. Their demands can be extremely strong and will be demonstrated in such ways as subtle or not so subtle comments, or even a slackening of attendance, or decrease in stewardship giving.

More and more, worship is turning into a form of entertainment as pastors give in to contemporary wants and needs of today's high-tech and fast-paced generations. This is not intended to suggest we stay stodgy or old-fashioned. But all the hype must not take over the quality and essence of what the church is all about. Keeping a balance is only possible when we as pastors remember what we are all about.

SCENARIO

Pastor Ron got a good laugh out of them with his joke that Sunday, and the people seemed so pleased. Nothing wrong with that! He had to admit he'd been a bit of a zealot in the past, probably because he was new to the parish ministry, and one very serious fellow. So, now, he'd taken the advice of a few church members and loosened up a bit. Ron had never been a theatrical type of person, but it occurred to him on that Sunday that he'd proven to have a pretty good sense of timing to get such a hearty laugh out of them.

As the weeks followed, Ron did his homework and came up with some very amusing things to say, even though his sermons still had sound theological content every Sunday. A few months later, he talked with the choir director about lightening up the music and picking up the tempos. Things were perking up as that year passed. Pastor Ron found he was spending more time seeking out material that would be entertaining and less time on his biblical studies. And, he admitted, at least to himself, that he was getting more popular with the young people.

It was just about the time when Ron was starting to enjoy his new persona that the worst happened. He was called before the council, out of the blue, and admonished. What they told him came as a surprise. "We called you to this church because we wanted to learn more about the Bible. We saw you as a serious young man with plenty to say that would make us better people. We know you still have that in you, and you can do it. But we want you to know that all those jokes are very distracting when we're trying to worship."

In time, Ron came to realize that, as important as it was to keep the people's attention, and as entertaining the rest might be, the message of the gospel was the most powerful thing he would ever have to offer them!

THEOLOGICAL REFLECTION

> I solemnly urge you: proclaim the message; be persistent whether the time is favorable or unfavorable; convince, rebuke, and encourage, with the utmost patience in teaching. (2 Tim 4:1b–2)

It is interesting to note that this Bible passage assumes that there are times that will not be favorable for preaching! Still, it is our calling to convince, rebuke, and always encourage with the utmost patience, in times that are good and bad! As much as we might be appreciated for the entertainment value of the words we preach, it is the message and the gospel content that count. Nothing could be more important. The people need to hear the word, the real nourishment, or they will go away hungry.

PRAYER

Great One, it is so tempting sometimes to turn your sanctuary into a place of entertainment instead of a house of worship. Certainly, you want us to be happy as your people and to be ourselves. Surely, our worship should be filled with joy and even sometimes with humor. But, there is so much more. There is deep joy, as well as the profound message of hope and life that your word brings. There are also the greatly needed moments of quiet reflection and spiritual uplifting. Help me, God, to discern what will work best for our people at each given time together, so that we may come to know you better, love you stronger, and be fulfilled by your presence in that holy place that we share together, our church.

I ask your holy guidance in the name of Jesus whose teachings were sometimes challenging, but always compelling.
AMEN

CHAPTER TWENTY-THREE.
Called to console, but am I consoling a perpetrator?

THE ISSUE

This topic is a tough one. It may not happen often in parish ministry, but it is possible you may have had this experience. A person comes to you for counseling and, as the person's story proceeds, you get the uneasy feeling that he or she is not telling you the whole truth. You even begin to wonder if the person may even be the perpetrator of the wrongdoing and not the victim or just the person talking about it. You feel nervous and uncomfortable. Should you do nothing, or do you need to act? If you did act, what on earth could you say? You can't make an accusation of any sort with nothing to back it up. But you just know that you feel suspicious and uneasy.

We are advised by Martin Luther that the real "church" on earth is composed of both saints and sinners, and that there is no real way for us to discern which is which. Our call is to serve the people who are put before us, the church members, and those related in some way to this church we serve. We do understand that it is not our task to judge them. But that doesn't mean we have to appease their bad behavior or go along with anything they might be doing of which we do not approve. Still, ultimately, it is God's work to judge them and not ours. How we respond to them will depend largely on whether they confess to us and if we know they have done wrong or not.

SCENARIO

Pastor Ken received the call from Adam, a church member, around four o'clock. Could he come over immediately to the pastor's office? Adam sounded very disturbed, so Ken felt he couldn't really say no. Adam arrived and was asked to sit down. He wept as he told Pastor Ken how upset he was with his niece Gina (whom he and his wife had been raising since she was a baby) and her new boyfriend. She had been getting bad grades in high school, he said, and showed a belligerent attitude toward both him and his wife. Pastor Ken listened attentively. Adam then asked him to pray for Gina that she would get rid of her current boyfriend and improve her attitude. Ken felt uncomfortable at many levels. Why was it that Adam had been so demanding with the details of the prayer Ken should give? How was Ken to know that this young woman needed this kind of prayer just because her uncle, Adam, was saying that she did? Pastor Ken did the best he could but chose to be more general in his words and prayed for that whole family. He also reminded Adam that he was only a pastor and not qualified to serve as a therapist, but that there were people who specialize in family dynamics who would be likely able to help. Adam, ready to leave, stood up suddenly, shook hands with Ken, and headed out of the office, still in tears. Ken could not put his finger on any reason, but he continued to feel incredibly uncomfortable. The feeling persisted as he made his way home and continued through the days that followed. This feeling the pastor had was, of course, only in his heart, because there was nothing he could appropriately prove or say or do. He did not sleep well for over a week. The idea kept coming back to him that the girl Gina's behavior as her uncle had described it seemed to indicate more that of a victim than of a deliberate troublemaker. And it kept coming to him also that her uncle Adam's searing tears and begging for prayer seemed to indicate something deeper than the appropriate reaction of a troubled patriarch. Right now, and maybe ever, nothing could be done, no action taken. Still, Pastor Ken remained uncomfortable and kept an eye on that family. Is it ever possible, he wondered to himself, that we pastors might be manipulated by a perpetrator? He felt guilty about his thoughts, which he considered must surely be unfounded. Still, we are haunted sometimes when our heart tells us something different from what our head tells us.

THEOLOGICAL REFLECTION

> When the son of man comes in his glory and all the angels with him, then he will sit on the throne of his glory. All the nations will be gathered before him, and he will separate people, one from another as a shepherd separates the sheep from the goats. And he will put the sheep at his right hand and the goats at the left. (Matt 25:31–33)

It is not possible for us, as pastors or as Christians, to always discern the righteous from the unrighteous. Human life is a complex business, and most people will fit into both of these categories at one time or another, or even at the same time, depending on circumstances and on chance. Ultimately, only God knows who constitutes the sheep and who are the goats, the righteous and the unrighteous. If we have good reason to suspect someone is hurting another person, then we are responsible both by law and conscience to take action to end the abuse. But, in the face of total ambiguity, all we can do is try to be faithful, keep our eyes open, and pray for clarity.

PRAYER

God, you know that I know it is only you who understands all things. You can rightfully and fully separate the good from the evil, the right from the wrong, the saint from the sinner. You also know, all too well, that I am only a human being. I can't be sure even when I'm right and when I'm wrong, when my judgment is "dead on" and when it is badly off the mark.

Give me judgment as only you can. Watch over my decision-making and my work with your beloved people. Please place me in situations where I can do the best good for all concerned. Guide me so I do not make mistakes or say things that are hurtful. Help me to interpret your word with the greatest care, so that your news is always ultimately good news for all concerned.

In the end, may your will be done. May every person turn away from evil ways and work ceaselessly for good to build your reign of love.

I ask this in the name of Jesus who calls us to ways of righteousness.

AMEN

CHAPTER TWENTY-FOUR.
Called to observe boundaries but afraid of being accused anyway!

THE ISSUE

Today, most pastors are trained in boundary issues, and for good reasons. In recent decades, case after case of sexual misconduct on the part of church workers and clergy has come into the public eye. In addition, there are situations in which the accusations are false, bringing great suffering to those who are wrongly accused. The matter of taking boundary training and such issues seriously cannot be overestimated.

We who are pastors generally feel strongly about our integrity, and we would be deeply hurt if anyone questioned our behavior, especially in matters related to sexuality. There are so many potential minefields in the parish ministry. The reason is that we are placed in a position of trust. Our position is also one of authority and power. Even though we do not see it that way, others may look to us as being in much more powerful positions than they.

SCENARIO

Richard had been a pastor for only two years, although he was not what you'd call a young man. He considered himself lucky (well, he meant "blessed") to have a church to serve, this being his second career. He was a bit confused and surprised when he learned in seminary about how careful he would have to be about what they called "boundary issues." He was educated about how a church is not always a safe place for anyone, but especially for women and youths and children who can be vulnerable to predators. He could hardly believe that human beings would be so selfish, cruel, and thoughtless. He understood as well as anyone that, because pastors are in a powerful position to some extent, their behavior has to be even more careful than that of others in the church.

This is the reason Richard was so unnerved and upset when he was accused of making undue advances toward a woman church member. From what he gathered, she was making a big issue out of their having bumped into each other in the church hallway. Richard was a happily married man and most certainly never had any undue thoughts, let alone actions, related to this woman. She, for whatever reason, saw it differently and was sure their bumping into each other was his deliberate action and that it constituted an inappropriate advance toward her. According to the woman, the pastor's body had touched hers in a way that she was sure he had enjoyed! She was angry and made it clear she wanted him removed from the church. She told her friends at church, and the word spread rapidly throughout the congregation. Should the gossip have been the end of it, Pastor Richard felt his reputation would still have been destroyed, so he was getting angry himself. Finally, the issue made its way to the church council and directly to Richard. He was embarrassed and mortified. That is when he learned very quickly that everyone needs an advocate because, even when innocent, we really cannot defend ourselves! Richard, fortunately, did have advocates in a small group of church members who defended him without condemning the accusing woman. They arranged for a small group to meet with Richard and the woman, separately, and then together, as both were willing to talk. As the talks proceeded, the accusing woman gradually backed off, admitting that she may have misunderstood what had happened between the two of them. She'd been having a hard time of it recently since the death of her beloved spouse. Richard explained that the day they bumped into each other, he had been worried about many things and distracted. He had not spoken to the woman but just acted as if she was not even there, and that was not good for a pastor. Richard was fortunate enough to have a spouse who trusted him with all her heart and supported his ministry. Things settled down in a relatively short time. Both the woman and Pastor Richard remained at the church. Richard felt very hurt at being accused and embarrassed in front of his congregation, but he was deeply relieved that this disturbance hadn't turned into anything bigger. In time, everyone seemed to forget that this nonevent had ever raised its head, and life at the church went on as usual. Richard knew too that, in far too many other circumstances, the pastor was both responsible and guilty.

THEOLOGICAL REFLECTION

> Keep back your servant [me] also from the insolent; do not let them have dominion over me. Then I shall be blameless and innocent of great transgression. (Ps 19:13)

One of the worst things that can happen to a person is to be unfairly accused of wrongdoing. In many instances in the Psalms, the psalmist is declaring innocence in the face of accusation. Exactly what these people are being accused of is never explained in the psalms. The reason may be that those who are unfairly accused have much in common, so the words prove true to us. In this psalm, the request to God is that the "insolent," presumably the accusers, should no longer hold power over the person.

When we are truly innocent of an accusation, it is important that we bring our feelings forward to God in prayer, and to anyone who can help us. Sometimes it is too easy for us to find ourselves totally innocent, so it is important in all circumstances of accusation that we really search our souls and be fair-minded as to what actually happened.

PRAYER

O God, you know all things. You protect the innocent and watch over those who are blameless. I have spent my life in the ministry working toward building your kingdom, teaching your message of love as best I know how, and also trying to protect the innocent. Yet, I worry so much that something could go wrong and even I might be accused one day. I follow all the rules and take special care to remember that sometimes people who are suffering from their own insecurities could blame me at any time for things I have not ever done or said. Help me to continue to do things always in a safe way while not losing my sense of trust for others and my ability to serve them with all my heart.

I pray too on this day for all those who have been hurt by predators in or out of the church setting. The deep suffering of so many people can seem overwhelming. And we seldom really know how to help. Give us strength to be useful to those who need us in these situations and to be a part of the bringing of justice.

When a woman was taken in adultery Jesus accused those who were about to punish her. Still, he also told her to go and sin no more (John 8:1–11). I pray in his holy name and remember how well he was able to forgive and love all sinners and yet call them to repentance.

AMEN

SECTION THREE

Choice, Actions, and Consequences

CHAPTER TWENTY-FIVE.
How can I know for sure that I'm in the right?

We all know that there are times we are simply not in the right. Most of us try to do right, especially if we are pastors. But, in real life and even in real ministry, it is not always clear what the right is! And that can be a problem!

SCENARIO

George had been a minister at this church for ten years when he came up with a magnificent idea. His idea was that they change the worship time from 10 a.m. to 9 a.m. and then offer Sunday school for the kids at 10, with adult educational opportunities available at that time as well. That way, whole families could worship together, the Sunday school teachers would be able to attend worship services, which had been impossible up to this time, and the adults would be more likely to get some additional Christian education while the children were in Sunday school. That way, they would not have to wait for them. Pastor George was absolutely convinced that he was right that this was a good plan. Unfortunately, it turned out that most of his congregation did not agree.

No amount of discussion, lecturing, subtle sermonizing, or chats at committee gatherings could seem to bring the congregation into agreement with George's great plan, although, throughout, he had very kindly and carefully explained everything. Clearly, they were not going to budge!

In time, Pastor George gave up on his master plan. He came to realize that, as perfect as his plan may well have been, it was not what the people wanted. Was he right or was he wrong? He would never know for sure.

Six years later, when he was serving another church, this same plan for a change in the Sunday morning worship time was brought up by a church member. George could hardly believe he was hearing this. And, this time, to his surprise, this church council not only sanctioned it, but the congregation voted approval. The plan went ahead. George never even mentioned to this new congregation that he had offered the same idea to his previous congregation to no avail. That would be his little secret. The plan went ahead speedily, and he pondered on how God works in mysterious ways. He also realized that something can be wrong for one group while being exactly right for another.

THEOLOGICAL REFLECTION

> Know then that God has put me in the wrong and closed his net around me. Even when I cry out "violence!" I am not answered; I call aloud, but there is no justice. (Job 19:6–7)

This is just one short example of Job's diatribe against God. He yells and he screams throughout the entire book of Job, telling God everything that he believes God is responsible for doing to both himself and others. He wants nothing less than justice, and he demands a hearing. This profound message reminds us that anger is a normal human emotion and that we are allowed to argue with Almighty God. It also tells us that God doesn't always respond in the way or in the time frame that we are demanding. God is still God, as God reminds Job, "Then the Lord answered Job out of the whirlwind . . . 'Where were you when I laid the foundations of the earth?'" (Job 38:1, 4).

Job is sure that he is justified in his anger because he knows he has followed all the rules. But, as all of us have learned, the world doesn't always operate according to the rules, and there is much that remains unaccounted for. Still, Job is a man who stands for and demands justice at least from his God. In God's good time, God returns to Job everything that he has lost.

How can we know when we're in the right? It is sometimes not even possible. But the best rule of thumb is to answer the question "Is it good news for everyone, not just for myself that I'm fighting for?" That will help us determine the better course. As pastors, we can assume we know what's best for our congregation, but it still may not be their choice of what they think best. We are at best guides, after all.

PRAYER

Mighty One, you always know when we are doing right and when we are wrong, but we are not always such good judges of that. You are the defender and protector of all who do right. Help me to know when I am right so that I may have the courage to continue, and when I am wrong so I can turn around.

In this world, O God, as you know, it is not so easy to discern right and wrong. There seem always to be so many gray areas, so much confusion, and so many interpretations of the given situation. Give me clarity, O Gracious One, so that I may do your will.

Help me to understand that there are many reasons why my congregation may not agree with my ideas, choices, or decisions. Help us to be your people together, like a family, working toward mutual goals. Teach me to learn from them, and teach them to learn from me.

I ask this in the name of the righteous one, who taught us that when we do not agree, we can still love each other, our brother, Jesus Christ.

AMEN

CHAPTER TWENTY-SIX.
What and how much am I willing to lose?

THE ISSUE

As we all know, there are times when we're expected to adjust our principles and give in to some issue we may not agree with, so we can keep ourselves in the fray! If we stand up for what we believe in, in the ministry as much as in any other working position, we may just find ourselves out the door and unemployed! Then, there is the issue of how a person gets the next position if let go from the previous one. It is serious business in any line of work to stand up for principles. In ordained ministry, it is perhaps even more serious, because integrity is what we are all about! No one wants a pastor who has compromised his or her principles to maintain a position. Yet, issues arise more often than we would like to admit, in which we, as pastors, are pushed to the brink.

SCENARIO

The church council of the Simms Avenue Church had taken a vote and decided to oust two outside groups who had been meeting at the church. One group was Parents of Troubled Teens that had been gathering there for over twenty years. The other group was a relatively new young mothers club. The official reasons were clear to the council, at least in their own eyes. The cost of heating and lights had gone up extensively in recent months, and it looked like neither group could afford to pay more than the minimal monthly "donation" they'd been making to the church out of funds gathered at each meeting. Pastor Sam was sincerely shocked at first that these groups were being asked to leave. Did the council members not see that both groups were offering a good service for the betterment of the community and for helping individuals? It was so obvious! These groups needed a place to meet. Besides, the one group had been coming there for so many years that it seemed simply wrong to push them out without a better reason. Aside from that, there was little use having an entire building that was hardly being used from Monday to Saturday. Pastor Sam found he was alone in the church most days of the week. The church numbers were down, and Sam felt it looked better if passersby would notice there were lights on, cars in the parking lot, and activity at the church during the week. Sam had expressed his strong opinions over recent weeks. Now that the vote was taken, it was clear the people had decided to pass over his recommendations as pastor, and simply do it their own way. Sam did understand that the council was the voting branch of the church membership and therefore had the full power to make this decision. But he, on the other hand, had been chosen as their spiritual leader. This matter had strong spiritual implications in his opinion—that is, helping others, being good stewards of the space, and helping to build up a better community.

Sam had to decide. Would he tell them, now that the vote had passed, how strongly he felt about this issue? If he went on about this after the fact, how much clout would he lose? How much respect would he lose or maybe gain? Would his "job" still be intact if he went against them? He decided for once he would do it. After seven full years as their pastor, he had always pretty much gone along with the decisions of the council. This time was different. He stood before them and said, "As your pastor, I feel it is only honest to say that I believe your decision was an unchristian one. When we start thinking about saving a few dollars on heat costs at the expense of an opportunity to meet people's needs, this cannot be right. When we ask a group that has found a home here for twenty years to leave, without even making preliminary efforts to find a way for them to stay, we are being selfish as a congregation. It is my sincerest wish that you will change your mind and not do this thing." Everyone was polite for the rest of the evening to Pastor Sam, but no changes were made. He went home that night and did some serious thinking about his congregation and about himself, and about what might be the will of God in this situation. Maybe Sam was the right pastor in the wrong place. Maybe some other pastor would be able to gain further respect from them, or deal with these kinds of issues in a different or better way. But, as much as Sam prayed and reasoned about the issue, he felt one thing strongly. It was wrong for the congregation to ask those groups to leave the church. In time, Sam decided to move on to a position in mission work. The matter of those two groups being asked to leave was never discussed further. The council did ask them to leave, and sadly they complied. Pastor Sam thought about this happening occasionally as the years passed, and wondered how much money, if any at all, the congregation had saved by asking those groups to leave the church.

THEOLOGICAL REFLECTION

> Then the word of the Lord came to him, saying, "What are you doing here, Elijah?" He answered, "I have been very zealous for the Lord, the God of hosts, for the Israelites have forsaken your covenant, thrown down your altars, and killed your prophets with the sword. I alone am left, and they are seeking my life, to take it away."
> (1 Kgs 19:9b–10)

In all the biblical texts, there are few if any people who are as zealous for the Lord as the prophet Elijah. In this passage, he is explaining to God what his reasons are, as well as the telling of the price he is expecting to have to pay for his zeal. The people have forgotten their promises to God, been disrespectful of the worship place, and even killed the people God has sent to help them. Elijah is clearly aware that the cost of his faithfulness to God may be his life, because he points out that they're trying to kill him.

We pastors are hardly likely to be in danger for our lives. Nevertheless, we're often in danger of losing many other things, from our reputation or popularity to our jobs and our incomes. The ways of the world are not always the ways of our faith.

Being the truly zealous type, it may not have been difficult for Elijah to decide which way to go. For us, things may not be so clear. Are we justified in standing up for justice, or are we sometimes just being stubborn and demanding? Is our point of view on a particular issue one that is clear cut in relation to biblical teachings, or might it be interpreted in a way that favors those who oppose us?

Our principles are an integral part of who we are. We are going to have to know what we stand for and how much we are willing to lose in order to maintain our dignity, our honor, and our principles. Often, we do not actually know until these are challenged, and we have much to lose. As tough as this may be, these times are the ones that offer us clear opportunities to shine and to prove, even to ourselves, what stuff we are made of and what is important in life. Nobody said the ministry would be an easy road.

PRAYER

God, lead me always in paths of integrity. Give me courage to know what "battles" to fight with all my heart, and which are less important. I understand it is usually difficult to see the forest for the trees. I can't always judge rightly when I am embroiled in these kinds of issues!

When I am stubborn, make me supple. When I am too sure that I am right, make me be sure to give fair consideration to the other side. If the time comes that I fear the disapproval of my people, help me to discern what is important and what is not.

I ask this in the name of Jesus who stood in strength against the enemy, who paid the price with his life, and who lives with you in glory.

AMEN

CHAPTER TWENTY-SEVEN.
Different responses to male and female pastors

THE ISSUE

After all these years, it is still a fact that female and male pastors are not always treated alike by the members of their church. It often begins when the person is called by a search committee. In many denominations, this committee presents the candidate to the congregation for a vote. If the candidate is a male, it is common for the person to receive a unanimous vote. After all, the people trust that the search committee has done its job. In the case of a woman pastor, however, a unanimous vote is rarely the case. Even though that committee has been given the responsibility to choose the new pastoral candidate, and even though the female candidate is fully qualified, totally delightful, and a great match for the church, the mere shock of her being a woman will likely mean she will receive some negative votes. People often do not admit, even to themselves, that this is their reason for a negative vote, so they will contrive other reasons. The woman will likely pass but with a lower percentage of approval by the congregation. This has changed quite dramatically over the years, but the issue has not yet come to an end.

Once settled in as a pastor, it continues to be difficult in some ways for a woman. Behavior that is thought of as strong and assertive in a man can be perceived, when in a woman, as pushy and

DIFFERENT RESPONSES TO MALE AND FEMALE PASTORS

aggressive. Women pastors are finding their place and, in many cases, are beloved. Still, the woman pastor walks a fine line and often must choose her words and actions very carefully!

SCENARIO

Pastor Gwen had been reluctant to attend seminary mainly because she had heard that women were not always welcome in the pulpit. At first, she could hardly believe that her sense of calling was legitimate, simply because she'd never even met a female pastor. But, in time, she did decide to take the plunge. Her years at the seminary were both fun and enlightening. She got good grades and made friends. By the time she graduated she had almost forgotten about her earlier concerns about being one of those women in ministry! She did quite well in finding a position as a pastor. It was as an associate, and she was aware that churches were more likely to choose a woman for this type of position, but she was new to ministry, so she felt she needed the experience before seeking a solo position.

Five years passed, and Gwen was more or less convinced that this whole issue of prejudice against women in ministry was simply not true. She'd been treated with love and respect pretty much and had no complaints. She also did not encounter the expected problems when she sought out a solo position. She was welcomed by everyone at the new church. It was weeks before Gwen had her first negative encounter with a church member. It was subtle; a few words spoken to her that could indicate a certain lack of respect if taken that way! Gwen decided, of course, to give the person the benefit of the doubt. When it happened again, with another church member, she felt a lot less comfortable. This congregation might simply be a different type from those she had served previously. The problem came to a head when a gathering of disgruntled members wanted to talk with her about an issue that was on their mind. Gwen was willing to talk with them about anything at all, but she also believed that things should go through due processes with the church council and be open to everyone on that council.

This small, unofficial group had chosen a leader and called her on a Friday just before 5 p.m. wanting her to meet with them on Tuesday afternoon. But they also refused to tell her what their agenda was for the meeting. The lack of respect she had suspected was turning out to be very real. Gwen was devastated, but she had to admit to herself that being a woman might have something to do with their behavior toward her.

Tuesday came, and the group walked into her office at the appointed time. What they had to talk to her about is not important. The main thing is that Gwen felt trapped by them and sensed strongly that their business with her was inappropriate. She'd had her reasons for not doing the thing they had wanted her to do, and they were good ones. She sat for over an hour trying to explain this to the group but wondered why she was even doing this. After all, who had appointed them to monitor her work?

That evening, Gwen sat down with her husband and shared some of the cruel and unreasonable words that had been said to her that day. His response surprised her. In his own life experience, he said, no person had ever spoken to him that way. He suggested to Gwen that at least part of what she was going through with this congregation may well have to do with the simple fact that she was a woman.

Did it? Would they have said those things to a male pastor—any male pastor? Gwen could never know for sure. There really was no way to ask them that question. It is possible that they themselves may not even have known the answer.

Prejudice against women pastors may be less common than in the past, but it is a reality. The reasons for this are hard to understand or explain. Gwen struggled through the issue at hand just as if the behavior of this group had nothing to do with her being a woman. She, of course, questioned herself and concluded after much prayerful consideration that she really had done nothing to deserve their treatment of her. She tried to love them through it and attempted to resolve the problem they had blamed on her. They arrived at some mutual agreement and, in time, most of them came to truly respect and love her. Gwen remembered, years later, how she had been warned early on, before she even entered the seminary, that it would not be easy for a woman. She'd chosen this path, and with God's help, made it this far. She was not about to stop now.

THEOLOGICAL REFLECTION

> There is no longer Jew or Greek; there is no longer slave or free; there is no longer male and female, for all of you are one in Christ Jesus. (Gal 3:28)

Parts of the Bible, of course, do reflect the imbalance between the sexes that was part of the culture of biblical times. But Jesus always treated women with equality. Here too, in the words of Paul, we find the glorious statement proclaiming total equality between male and female! This equality, unfortunately, is still not a full reality in the world we live in. We are working at it, but the progress is slow and the work is tedious.

PRAYER (FOR WOMEN PASTORS)

God, you knew what you were doing when you made me a woman! And, heaven knows, I am so happy to be one! We women, as you know, have the joy of bringing new life into the world. And, whether or not we ourselves bear children, we seem somehow hardwired to nurture the world! So many people depend on me at this time of my life. I pray with all my heart that you will give me the strength to deal with all the nonsense that goes on related to my being a woman pastor. Find ways for the people who don't know how to deal with my womanhood (both men and women!) to understand that I am as accomplished, as faithful, and as good a religious leader as any man they might have chosen to be their pastor. I say this in humility.

I am well aware that, in our country and in our culture, women ministers are still a relatively new idea. Give me patience to be a good role model and a faithful servant of your word for those women who will follow me. Help me to keep cool when people say the wrong things. Guide me to be proactive for my rights and the rights of other women without losing my idealism and sense of goodness and generosity toward others.

I pray all this in the name of Jesus who always supported woman's equality and who had followers and friends who were women.

AMEN

CHAPTER TWENTY-EIGHT.
Can everybody win, and, if not, who needs to win?

THE ISSUE

There was, a few decades ago, a very popular book entitled *I'm OK, You're OK* by Thomas A. Harris. It begs the question, does there have to be a good guy and a bad guy in every situation? And, secondly, is it possible for both sides to win? Hence, we have the expression "win-win" situation. Of course, the answers depend on each individual circumstance. Still, there can be some general truths in this regard. To begin with, is it naïve to suggest that in many situations of difficulty, there is no person who is intentionally doing evil? Often, misunderstandings are the cause of friction, and resolutions can come with even a minimum of honest dialogue.

It is part of the human condition to want to be the winner but, in the ministry, consensus and mutual agreement are better to be sought after than being right while others are wrong.

SCENARIO

Pastor Marco had been in an ongoing disagreement with this church member Lorne for over two years now. They'd never had it out exactly, but he was afraid the others were starting to notice the icy feelings being exchanged between them.

The trouble with Lorne, as Pastor Marco saw it, was that he was one of those people who seemed to have to be right all the time. Lorne had bullied his way through multiple church controversies, many of which, according to Marco's thinking, were created by Lorne himself. Lorne had broken the lawn mower and insisted on having the church buy a new riding mower that they could ill afford. Then he wanted to be the one to ride it! Lorne had planted six flowering trees in front of the church without the permission of the council, and later demanded they get special pruning and fertilization twice a year from a particular nursery. Lorne had doggedly pushed through changes in the way they practiced communion, and later complained about how the elders were serving it. The list went on from there.

Certainly, Lorne had no reason to complain because he always seemed to win. But this time he was going directly against the will and desire of Pastor Marco. His son was going to be confirmed, and Lorne wanted the confirmation class group to meet on Saturday evenings, when it was more convenient for him to drive the boy over to the church, instead of the Wednesday evenings that Pastor Marco had planned and arranged.

Pastor Marco dug in his heels this time and decided he was not going to change everyone else's schedule just so good old Lorne could win one more time. Lorne started calling him at home in the evenings about it, and eventually even went to the education committee to try to get his way. Marco felt he might be acting in a somewhat un-pastoral manner, but he kept on saying, "No. Wednesday evenings sound good." He certainly didn't want to be teaching a group of teenagers the night before he had his Sunday service, and he was also sure kids had other things to do on Saturday night than come to confirmation class. Besides, he liked to spend that one night, Saturday, with his own family. Clearly, he and Lorne were at loggerheads!

Finally, after Marco had been praying about it and thinking about it and stewing over it and getting nowhere, his wife Andrea came up with an idea. Why not another day, neither the day Marco had chosen nor the day Lorne had insisted on? Marco did not like the idea at first, because he was getting a bit stubborn about it himself. Besides, he told Andrea, Lorne would never go for it. Still, he gave Lorne a call and said, "What about Tuesday nights for confirmation?" To his surprise, after some hesitation, Lorne said he thought Tuesday nights should work for his son, and, after checking with the other youths, it was a go!

The point was not that Lorne hadn't won, but that he had not lost. Clearly Lorne had some growing to do. It was not a clear victory for Marco; that's for sure. But Marco consoled himself with the thought that this man Lorne must have led a difficult life. Lorne seemed to have a lot of winning he needed to do in order to feel good about himself. Besides, maybe this time Lorne had moved one step closer to putting others above himself. It was a tie!

THEOLOGICAL REFLECTION

> Then, the king said, "The one [woman] says, 'This is my son who is alive, and your son is dead,' while the other says, 'Not so! Your son is dead, and my son is the living one.'" So, the king said, "Bring me a sword," and they brought a sword before the king. The king said, "Divide the living boy in two; then give half to the one, and half to the other." But the woman whose son was alive said to the king, because compassion for her son burned within her, "Please, my lord, give her the living boy; certainly, do not kill him!" The other said, "It shall be neither mine nor yours; divide it." Then the king responded: "Give her [the first woman] the living boy; do not kill him. She is his mother." (1 Kgs 3:23–27)

We are raised and educated to believe that, in every court case, it is right that one side wins and the other must lose. Still, in too many situations of conflict, once resolved, both sides lose in one way or another. In this story, if one of the so-called mothers had won full custody of the child, that would be good only if she were the true mother. If the judge had indeed cut the child in half, of course, both mothers would have lost! The answer to the question "Who needs to win?" is most obvious in this story but not always so clear in contemporary life. Still, it's a very important question for us to ask ourselves as pastors whenever we are involved in conflict. It's perfectly natural for us to want to win, but in the interest of Christian love, it may be that the other person or group needs the win much more than we do.

PRAYER

God of all creation, you created us to care for and love each other. Yet so often we don't get along. There is conflict in our world, conflict between our own political parties, among our own acquaintances and friends—and sometimes even within our own families. Is it possible, O Great One, that we are simply not listening to each other? Why are we not willing to consider the reasons why the other person or group holds that opinion, or acts that way? Could it be, O God, that the person who always seems to disagree with me is suffering in some way that I cannot imagine or do not see?

Help me to realize that I can be wrong too. And, if I chance to actually be right, guide me to know that being right is not always the most important thing. Give me patience with those who disagree with me. Grant me a heart that can truly love those who set themselves up as my adversaries. And give me strength, when I am truly convinced that they are wrong, to be willing to try my best to turn their hearts to the ways of good.

I know we live in an imperfect world and that there will be times that we clash with others. Still, dear God, if there can be a "win-win" here, help me to make that happen. As the famed prayer of St. Francis of Assisi states, "Lord, make me an instrument of your peace. Where there is hatred, let me sow love; where there is injury, pardon."

I ask this in the name of the one who is named the Prince of Peace, Jesus of Nazareth.

AMEN

CHAPTER TWENTY-NINE.
Can I live with occasionally being the "bad guy"?

THE ISSUE

Naturally, obviously, we think when we become a pastor that we are going to be a sort of resident good person in our congregation and our community. We'll be role models for the rest. Of course, we know we're far from perfect. Inside, we may even think that we're the worst of the sinners, but on the outside, we can shine for them. We'll obey God's laws and do what is right.

As I suspect many of you already have learned, this part of our ministry is not always so easy and at times not even possible. Sometimes we find ourselves seen by one, by many people in the congregation, or even by the larger community, as the "bad guy."

SCENARIO

It was Good Friday. Normally, Pastor Mary looked forward to this day. As melancholy a day as it was, theologically speaking she, like her fellow Christians, also knew that Easter would follow on Sunday. Mary had been invited in this particular Lenten season to participate in the community Good Friday worship service. As fate would have it, or at least as her colleague pastor had arranged it, it turned out that Pastor Mary was chosen to read the words of Pontius Pilate. Out of her mouth would be uttered the words that condemned Jesus to be crucified. She was also instructed to join in with the other pastors in cruelly shouting the words "Crucify him! Crucify him!" There was not a big crowd this year. Fewer and fewer people every year were attending these ecumenical services. Mary took the time while others were speaking to look around and see who from her congregation had chosen to attend. But she hadn't seen them all. Just when she walked up to the lectern to read the words that would condemn Jesus, she happened to look at the congregation and over to the left. There in the second pew sat three people, holding hands, wearing black, and looking bereft. She could hardly believe her eyes. At the center of the three was Melanie, her Sunday school supervisor whom she, just last week, had fired—the only person she had ever fired! Flanking Melanie on either side were her two young children, a boy of nine and a girl of ten: all three looking forlorn. In that split second after seeing them, she had to read her lines. Pastor Mary composed herself as best she could and read the words of Pilate. Then she sat down in silence and asked herself, "Are they sad because Jesus has been condemned to die? Or are they sad because Melanie lost her job and they won't have enough money to get along?" The three glared at her and quietly wept. A third possibility also crossed her mind, and it was this: "Did that woman bring her children here all dressed in black to put on a show just to upset me for firing her?" Then, Mary realized it was her turn to join the other leaders and shout, "Crucify him. Crucify him!" Of course, she didn't let it show, but her mind and heart were racing. She realized for the first time how ordinary good people can get caught up into being the bad guy, with little or no recourse. Scripture suggests that Pilate was reluctant to sentence Jesus to death, even saying to the crowds that this man is innocent. Yet, in the end, he went ahead and didn't stop the process. "Today I am the bad guy," Mary said to herself. "Today I learn a hard lesson. This is what it feels like to hurt people and to have little recourse." Mary had been told by church members that Melanie had shouted at parents more than once. Melanie had also, in words that were somewhat less than clear, actually threatened to harm Mary. It had seemed the right thing to do to let her go, for the good of the church, and of course Mary had to be the one to do it.

There are tough things one has to do as a pastor, and there are difficult decisions that must be made. Pastor Mary had weighed the options about firing this woman for weeks. She had considered the possible consequences of her decision, for the congregation, for individuals in the congregation, and for Melanie who would lose her job. She had thought about the church's future, about Melanie's future, and about what God would want her to do. Most importantly, Mary had weighed the matter with the appropriate committees, and the decision had been a mutual one. Nevertheless, it had come down to this. Her good decision had been painful for the woman she fired and possibly also for her family. That was a fact for Pastor Mary that could not be denied. Consequently, for Melanie and her family, Mary was the villain, and she'd simply have to live with it! The decision to let Melanie go had not been that of Pastor Mary alone, but she alone would bear the responsibility.

THEOLOGICAL REFLECTION

> If they have called the master of the house Beelzebul, how much more will they malign those of his household! (Matt 10:25b)

In this most interesting passage, Jesus suggests that he has been maligned and is telling the disciples it's very likely that his followers will be similarly maligned. Being viewed as the "bad guy" can happen to a person even when doing the right thing, when standing up for what is right or sticking to convictions. This is especially the case when we are going against the popular ways of the world. One might say it "goes with the territory."

Jesus had to take heavy criticism from the religious leaders of his day because he was willing to suggest their interpretations of Scripture didn't always go along with their ways of life. Jesus was ultimately arrested, convicted, and crucified as a common criminal, along with two real criminals.

In this passage, we are warned that we may occasionally have to pay the price of unpopularity for our convictions and for the actions we take.

PRAYER

God, how did I get into this mess? I've had to make a decision that may have to hurt someone. You know perfectly well that I went into the ministry to be a good person, a role model for the people. Okay, I'll admit it. I also hoped that the congregation I served would love me. After all, I love them. It was not my intention to ever have to hurt anyone or even fire somebody. Big business decisions like that come from business executives, and they seem to be able to do it with impunity. But my role in the church is about love, about hope, about forgiveness, about happiness. Help me to figure out how I can reconcile this thing I have had to do.

Give me the strength to understand that living and being a leader in this world is not always easy or decision-free. It's not so much that I want to justify my decision but rather that I want to live with it and face the fact that these things come up from time to time and I will have to be strong.

One more thing, my rock and my redeemer! Do not let me become unaware of any possible suffering on the part of others that is caused by my decisions. Help me live with what I have done (what I feel I have had to do) with courage, but never lose my sensitivity to others.

Most of all, Great One, I ask you to guide me into making right decisions, those that build up your church and your reign.

I know the expression "What would Jesus do?" may have become a cliché, yet I want to keep on asking that question, in his holy name.

AMEN

CHAPTER THIRTY.
What if issues are "swept under the carpet"?

THE ISSUE

One secret that most pastors don't know is that many churches live in the presence of ghosts. These are the ghosts of ministers who have long been gone and may even be dead, and also the ghosts of bad events and poor relationships past, all swept carefully and quite deliberately under the carpet by congregations, often even for generations.

When we come to serve a church as pastor, we are aware that (in most cases) we are not the first. We understand intellectually that most of the people have been served by other pastors before us. But, at some emotional level, we believe that, for them as well as for us, our arrival is the mark of new beginnings. When we arrive, we hope, pray, and expect that what happened in the past is gone forever and we have a clean slate. This is rarely the case.

Churches have histories, and so much about them is conditioned by those histories. These histories are sometimes related to us but, more often, changed to put everyone in a better light and, sometimes, swept so far under the carpet that everyone seems to have forgotten they ever happened! Many churches have secrets that continue to fester and burn beneath the surface for generations. The reason this can happen in churches is that church is the place where everyone wants things to be "nice," all behavior to be "Christian," and all memories to be happy ones! Life has a way of messing up our beautiful scenarios and best laid plans. Church is no exception.

So, if you suspect there is some under-the-surface problem from the past causing havoc or at least difficulty in your congregation, look to the past. One of the easiest ways to recognize such a problem is that you are being a fine and honorable pastor, but people are still indicating a certain discomfort around you. You may feel there is a sense of distrust among individuals or committees toward you or each other. It might very well be that their behavior indicates a general sense of distrust of the clergy. This behavior may be directed toward you but reflect a time in the past when an earlier pastor proved to be untrustworthy or irresponsible. When a congregation finds itself in a situation of having chosen a pastor who is less than worthy, that congregation often has decided to save face. They may never have openly admitted their mistake or the pastor's faults to the community or possibly even to each other. They were embarrassed. Sometimes they had let the pastor go or that pastor had been encouraged to take early retirement. Or they may even have kept the pastor for many years. The point is that in these cases the people tried to resolve the problem by hiding it rather than dealing with it openly. For this reason, the problem remains beneath the surface and waits there until any opportunity arises to bring it up again. You may become the brunt of such an issue and be the last person to know. When such a thing happens, you can start with putting away blame. This will free you up to be more useful in facing the issue. With the facts clarified, you can get things cleared up and go forward in your ministry to this congregation. The hardest thing in such situations, however, is to get the people to see and admit what the problem is really about!

SCENARIO

Pastor Rick could not figure out why his congregation didn't seem to trust him. After all, they had chosen him out of over twenty candidates and assured him that his credentials were top flight. He'd served two churches before, one as youth minister and the other as an associate in a team of four. He'd been excited about finally being a senior pastor and felt he was prepared and well qualified at this time of his life. Before going into the ordained ministry, he had worked as a business manager, so Rick was nobody's fool. He liked to think he knew people and he knew the church.

When he had asked the older church members about their history, they nearly always talked about parties they had enjoyed together, trips to church-related summer camps, various ministries they'd engaged in and such. When he asked them about their previous pastors, they nearly always seemed to talk a little faster. Some would look away and give him general information instead of any details. One pastor had served seventeen years, they told him, and the one immediately before Rick had retired early due to an illness, after serving for eight years. Rick decided to do a small investigation. It was like pulling teeth, and of course he had to be subtle and delicate with his questions. He noticed that nobody seemed willing to give him a direct answer. After a few weeks of giving it his best shot, and also checking with people in the community from outside the church, Rick began to put the pieces together. What he learned was shocking.

The earlier pastor who had been there for seventeen years had a strong personality and an equally powerful ego, as the stories about him went. He wanted to control everyone in the church. He had, it appeared, used his personality to overpower everyone who got in his way. So, for the entire seventeen years, what he wanted was what was done. The people had gradually become submissive to his will. Even though the denomination was one that encouraged self governance and lay leadership, these had gone by the wayside to appease the powerful pastor! It seemed also that people did not particularly like him, but that he had not even noticed. In other words, the church had revolved around him. The pastor that followed, Rick's predecessor, had inherited this environment and basically carried on being the sole power holder. Committees were weak or nonexistent. The people had chosen him because, it seems, they had lost their voice.

All this was reason enough for the congregation to distrust Rick, but there was something worse. When things are swept under the carpet, there is generally good reason! Dust is dirty! This last pastor had taken his power-tripping beyond the pale. That man had engaged in a two-year affair with a woman church member, even though he was a married man. And, to make things worse, he had been accused of inappropriate advances toward a second woman while on a pastoral visit to her home to visit her aged and very sick mother. Word of all this had come out slowly but steadily over the years that he was their pastor. At first, the congregation had been afraid to speak at all. In time, it all did come out. That was the time to face and deal with the facts. Fact one: They had been fooled over the many years into believing they were powerless, and they had bought into this lie. Fact two: They had chosen yet another power wielder so they would not have to take responsibility. Fact three: This next pastor had gone beyond the bounds of decency, and they had also let that go on for far too long! Instead of openly facing the reality of their congregation's sad situation, they covered it up. Their meetings on the issue were held in secret. They assured each other that the best thing to do was to see that pastor out the door with some believable excuse such as health issues and early retirement as being his own choice. They ended up offering him a rather good retirement package and sent him packing. "What's to be lost?" they said. "He can get out of here with his dignity intact and we can start running this place ourselves."

And that is just what happened. Unfortunately, that pastor went to another church where he repeated the harmful behavior he had not had to account for earlier. And, as for the church, the people turned from being far too docile to being much too dominating. And, now, poor innocent Pastor Rick had inherited the whole mess.

Was this issue ever resolved? Yes, but only after many tears and many heart-rending meetings in which matters of the past had to be brought to light. Naturally, we can't recreate the past, so there was some disagreement on what had transpired. It was a full four years of talk and dealing with one trust issue at a time, before Rick had helped the congregation to really put this matter to rest and begin again his own genuine ministry with them. But this time, the dust was swept into the dustbin and carried right out of the church. The church was clean both on top of the carpet and underneath it! Both Rick and his people could breathe.

THEOLOGICAL REFLECTION

> Nothing is covered up that will not be uncovered and nothing secret that will not become known. Therefore, whatever you have said in the dark will be heard in the light, and what you have whispered behind closed doors will be proclaimed from the housetops. (Luke 12:2–3)

Jesus is speaking here in relation to the hypocrisy of some religious leaders of his time. His words remind us that, with God there are no secrets. He is also saying that if we have words or actions worth doing then they should be done in the open.

Secrets are sometimes kept for very long times, even for generations. The strange thing about them is that, in many cases, it is surprising how many people know them, and how very harmful they can be. Secrets are often the cause for people's being treated poorly without reason. Secrets are the reason we may make wrong decisions, because we don't have all the information we need. Secrets have hurt people; secrets that too often have been kept in the interest of protecting the perpetrators.

There is no excuse for a congregation to cover up the misbehavior of a pastor or any church members of the past. It happens too often at the expense of the church's ability to move forward. Jesus says that everything that is in the dark will be revealed in the light. Once things are out in the open, they become much less ominous and we can often deal with them, thus ending all kinds of worry and suffering. Many businesses have learned this the hard way. It is time now for the church to do the same.

PRAYER

God, you know all things from past and present. You can see and judge all of us and our behavior. You also know our hearts: our intentions, our motivations, and our reasons for what we do. But it is not true that we can do the same. We hardly know ourselves, let alone others. We rarely know when people do us harm, whether they meant ill in their hearts or may just have been stupid or thoughtless. Likewise, when they do good things for us, we can never be sure that they did it for love. There are so many selfish reasons why they might have done these good things for us. So, today, Mighty One, I pray for the gift of discernment. What a gift it is! And should I receive the ability to better discern good from ill, may that knowledge be for the good of the church and for all concerned. If someone's intention is ill, help me to help that person to turn around and do your will. If their plan is for my good, then help me to be grateful. Guide me to be useful to them in turn.

And bless the church I serve. Churches are so delicate, dear God. They are holy, but they consist only of flawed and imperfect humankind. Help me to serve them with honor. If they are troubled, help me to find out what might be their painful reasons. May every church be focused on doing your will on earth, to your glory and in the service of helping others. Together, let us help make a better world.

I ask all this in the name of Jesus, who had such a gift for understanding all of our human failings, and who loves us till the end.

AMEN

CHAPTER THIRTY-ONE.
When the retired pastor will not leave

THE ISSUE

It seems perfectly logical that a pastor who reaches retirement age then would be not only willing but anxious to set aside the heavy responsibilities of the parish ministry, leave the work of the church to the newly appointed pastor, and move happily into the role of retiree in some other location. Unfortunately for all concerned, this is very often not the case. Many pastors do not realize that they have become almost addicted to the work they have been doing, even if that work is very difficult and often frustrating. The reasons for this are manifold, but they can include such matters as being highly respected and admired, having become the center of attention, feeling needed in serious decision-making situations, and such. Whether a retiring pastor gets in the way of the incoming one is of course a matter of that pastor's personality, so there are varying degrees of trouble in relation to this issue. And, of course, different denominations view this matter in different ways. Still, in general, it is better that the pastor who is leaving duties in a congregation should move on to worship and be a member in another church. Otherwise, it can be almost impossible for the new leader to take his or her place as the genuine pastor there. It is unfortunate but true that these pastors who just do not leave are often not doing this interfering on purpose. They might think they are leaving but then it just doesn't happen. They may genuinely believe they are needed for some kind of transition period, thinking they have been invaluable, and that the congregation cannot function without them. The neediness is almost if not always on their part and not that of the congregation. The new pastor does not want to be impolite and too often allows them to stay simply to keep the peace. The innocent congregational members keep calling their beloved old pastor requesting that they perform baptisms and marriages and funerals, leaving the new pastor little chance to even participate in the important events of people's lives.

SCENARIO

Pastor Barbara had served as an associate pastor for six years in another state, and now she had been called to serve her first church as the solo pastor. It was a rather large congregation of about six hundred, and she could hardly contain her joy. Once she and her husband had comfortably moved to the new location, it was time to begin her new ministry. She began to meet the parishioners over the first few weeks and to attend committee meetings and make hospital visits. It was good. She could feel the beginnings of warm relationships between herself and the people. But she began also to hear more and more about their "wonderful" pastor who had retired. He'd been there for eighteen years and had chosen to retire at sixty-four years of age, following kidney surgery. He had called her and suggested he should maybe stay away for six weeks and then return to worship. She agreed that it could be a good idea. It was not long before she realized that he and his wife had been close friends with three of the couples who seemed to be pillars of this congregation. Then she learned from the grapevine that his wife and the two other wives from the church were walking on the beach three mornings a week. It was not long before Pastor Barbara was convinced that the previous pastor was continuing to influence the leaders of the congregation to the point that they were following his lead in most every issue that came up.

When the six weeks were up, she called him and suggested he should stay away for longer, and he reluctantly agreed. Still, it became, over the first year, almost useless for her to make suggestions. She felt sure everything she did for the congregation was "vetted" by that retired pastor. In the meantime, she was also hearing some hints that his behavior had not always been entirely appropriate. She had no proof of this, so there was nothing to be done. He wanted to come back, and she could strongly sense this would not work for any of them. He needed to go to another church! He insisted on their meeting at another church to discuss it, and this was arranged. They met five times for hours at a time, with no results. Neither at this point would budge.

After five long years of trying to be the real pastor of that congregation, Pastor Barbara decided it was time for her to move on. That church had eleven retired pastors from other churches and even other denominations as current members Being aware of Pastor Barbara's dilemma, they got together with her for a chat. They informed her that they were going to write a kind letter to their retired pastor suggesting strongly that he move on and join another congregation in the area as soon as possible. To everyone's surprise, he agreed. So, as things turned out, it was not only their pastor, Barbara, but also their retired pastor who moved on to serve another church.

THEOLOGICAL REFLECTION

> Now the Lord said to Abram, "Go from your country and your kindred and your father's house to the land that I will show you." . . . Abram was seventy-five years old when he departed . . . . Abram took his wife Sarai and his brother's son Lot . . . and they set forth to go to the land of Canaan. (Gen 12:1–5)

Here, in the first book of the Hebrew Scripture, God is asking a person to just go forward in trust, not knowing what the outcome will be. Abram's life from that point becomes quite an adventure.

And this can be for any of us who moves into the future without a guaranteed outcome or even a plan. The retired pastor in this scenario felt that he did know how things would be for him if he remained in his old church. To join another congregation would have put him in the position of just being one more church member. Still, with his pastoral experience, he could have been very useful in a new situation without bringing a challenge to a new pastor just beginning to spread her wings.

PRAYER

Dear God, it must be that you brought me here for some good reasons. Why am I not getting a chance to simply be their leader without everything I do being questioned? If you want me to learn some lesson from this, believe me, I am learning fast. Help me to get through this stage of my ministry here, if indeed it is just a stage. I do not want to leave, because I have not even had a real chance to begin. I want to be their pastor—their real and genuine pastor. And, yes, I would love it if they could start to love me the way they loved and honored him.

God, please know that deep in my heart, I do wish him well. (Yes, to be honest I also wish him gone, at least from this congregation, but I do wish him well.) May he go somewhere where he finds joy in his new lay ministry and where he and his wife can find new friends just as good and faithful as the ones he has had here. I wish him health and a long life. But I would also like a chance to do the job to which they called me, and to be their real and complete pastor and leader. Help us both, O God. Help us in Jesus' name.

AMEN

CONCLUSIONS.
Thank God I am called

We are all aware of the fact that ordained ministry is never easy. Our work has its rewards, but it is also challenging in almost all cases. Chances are that, even after suffering through all the troubles of being a pastor, you still maintain a strong sense of your calling from both God and the church. That calling is deep and binding. Being chosen, in biblical terms, always means to be chosen for a task, and nobody said ministry would be a bed of roses. But you have been chosen and what a calling it is!

If we take some time on a regular basis to think of all the positive aspects of the great work we do, it won't take long before we start feeling really blessed. One particularly important aspect is the fact that what we are doing every day touches so many lives. We interact with God's precious people in the world at their times of greatest need and at the times of their greatest joy and their deepest suffering: weddings, baptisms, funerals, confirmation day, just to name a few. We celebrate with them the most important days of the year in a religious sense as well: Christmas and Easter and the rest. We help couples raise their children. With them we are creating and nurturing genuine community. We go with them into the world to make a difference. And, maybe most important of all, we teach and preach the word of God. In whatever ways our specific denominations go about doing that, it is we, the pastors, who help them discern the message that builds abundant life. Who could ever have a better "job" than that? We have so much for which to be thankful.

SCENARIO

Harvey was celebrating today. It was the thirtieth anniversary of his ordination. The congregation he was presently serving was his fourth. It was far from perfect, but, with the experience he had acquired over the years, he could handle everything with a modicum of grace. The people liked him enough to have planned a nice dinner and party at the church hall, and Harvey and his spouse Grace were going to thoroughly enjoy this event.

The party went well. Various people gave short speeches and reminisced on times they and Pastor Harvey had shared. This was, of course, only a part of Harvey's thirty-year ministry remembrance. When the party was over, he and his dear Grace sat down in the quiet of their own living room and continued the reminiscence. They talked about their early days, his decision to go into the ministry, the time at seminary, and all four churches he had served. They laughed that night about things that had seemed hardly laughing matters back when they were happening. Then they cried together as they remembered so much of the suffering that ordained ministry had meant to both pastor and pastor's family. And then they washed a few dishes together and went to bed. It has been said that life is pain, loneliness, worry, boredom, and sadness, but it's over too soon! You might say the same of ordained ministry. They had spent a lifetime in the ministry (his ministry and her unending support of it), and they agreed that they were not sorry! God had worked along with them all along the road, and what an exciting and fulfilling road it had proven itself to be.

THEOLOGICAL REFLECTION

> He has told you, O mortal, what is good, and what does the Lord require of you but to do justice and to love kindness, and to walk humbly with your God? (Mic 6:8)

Yes, you're called to the ministry but, in the end, what is required of you is not different from a person in any other work or calling. Do justice. Love kindness or mercy. Walk in humility with your God. Listen to the simplicity and truth of these words! Doing justice is never easy, but we who are good people are always moving in that direction, even when things don't go as planned or smoothly. Secondly, we are not called to simply do kindness or mercy or compassion. Rather, we are asked to love these things. They have to be important to us if we're going to serve God with integrity. And, thirdly, the text does not suggest that we will be alone in doing this work. No, the passage says we are to walk in humility, but we will not be alone; we walk with each other, and with our God beside us all the way.

PRAYER

God of Love and Compassion, I humbly come into your presence with thanksgiving. I am so grateful, O Wonderful One, for all you have done for me. Even though I've had my ups and downs all these years, I am so thankful that you called me to be a pastor. It is certainly quite different from what I had thought it would be when I went to the seminary. I find I have often been so busy I could not be as perfectly prepared as I would have hoped to be. I know there have been times I've said the wrong things and done the wrong things.

Have I been a decent pastor, God? I think in the big picture I did pretty well, but I am aware that people can always fool themselves. Either way, God, I do want you to know it was always my intention and my desire to do my very best for your church. So, for what I've done that was wrong, or what I have left undone that I should have done, I sincerely ask your forgiveness.

Help me not to focus on those mistakes now, but to rejoice in and truly celebrate my ministry. Help me to really forget any bad times in time and to put away the sad times. Teach me to laugh and live in the memory of the good times, and yes even the great times.

Thank you, God, for making me a pastor. Help me through the years ahead as you have always done in the past. Bless every member of the churches I have served. Bless my family who has lived through this ministry as much as I have. And, as you have promised, bless and watch over me.

I ask this in the name of Jesus who was always the people's rabbi (teacher), minister, friend, and savior.

AMEN

SOME LAST THOUGHTS

Together, we have walked through a wide variety of classic pastoral situations. We've had a chance to think about the fact that, whatever our situation, it is very likely we are not alone. Many of these situations come up with many pastors! Knowing this, hopefully, we can continue to see our ministry in a positive light even during the more difficult times. Ordained ministry is highly challenging but deeply rewarding work. We have read a short story or scenario that describes each situation in some detail. We've considered a related biblical passage and done some theological reflection. Then, for each situation, we have given a prayer. Naturally, your personal issues will be different in some or many ways from what has been presented here. Still, the general issues do not change that much. And, of course, there will be wording in your own prayers that will be different from those you have read. As we said early on, these prayers are offered more to get our own conversations with God started. Still, it may be that parts of the text will give us direction or focus for our own personal prayers.

It is probable that no job or career in the world turns out to be exactly what a person expects it to be. This is certainly true of the parish ministry. Every day brings new challenges and sometimes even problems that seem insurmountable. Yet, we have come this far. And we do not tread this road alone. Even in those days when there is no person that we can appropriately talk to about our worries, we have a strong sense that, in ministry, God is always with us. As we have learned, God is not likely to step in directly and solve problems for us (and God never promised to do such a thing). God's promises are more subtle, but God walks with us. Like the travelers on the road to Emmaus, we don't always recognize when

Jesus is walking alongside us, urging us to look to Scripture when we have troubles and sadness and problems. It's all there and has been all along, Jesus says (Luke 24:27). He is also with us in "the breaking of the bread" (Luke 24:35) and the sharing of the cup.

It is this author's deepest hope, in the writing of this book, that you will have found some sense of God's presence, of not being alone in your ministry's more difficult times, and that you will have also found help or direction in ways of thinking about dealing with these problems that come along with the work that we do.

ADDENDUM.
If you feel overwhelmed

There are times for many in parish ministry when the circumstances seem emotionally too much to bear. Be assured that when that happens there is always help. Aside from sharing with family or trusted friends if appropriate, there are also support networks and confidential lines of care. These are often offered at little or no charge. These people will (most importantly) listen to your troubles, stand by you, and guide you on how to move in good directions. For such assistance, it is recommended you contact the offices of your own denomination. If this is not working, your primary care physician should be able to help you. Any level of depression can become progressively more serious. So, if you sense that you need help, now is the time to act. No matter what your situation, listen to your instincts. You are urged to get help now. The work that you do impacts so many others. Become the best you can be, so that you and the people you serve can continue to grow in faith and rejoice in all that church life can bring!

www.ingramcontent.com/pod-product-compliance
Lightning Source LLC
Chambersburg PA
CBHW031459160426
43195CB00010BB/1024